NECESSARY DISTANCE

NECESSARY DISTANCE

ESSAYS AND CRITICISM

Clarence Major

COFFEE HOUSE PRESS

COFFEE HOUSE PRESS is an independent nonprofit literary publisher
supported in part by a grant provided by the Minnesota State Arts
Board, through an appropriation by the Minnesota State Legislature,
and in part by a grant from the National Endowment for the Arts.
Significant support for this project came from an anonymous donor.
Support has also been provided by Athwin Foundation; the Bush
Foundation; Elmer L. & Eleanor J. Andersen Foundation; Honeywell
Foundation; James R. Thorpe Foundation; Lila Wallace-Reader's Digest
Fund; McKnight Foundation; Patrick and Aimee Butler Family
Foundation; Pentair, Inc.; The St. Paul Companies Foundation, Inc.;
the law firm of Schwegman, Lundberg, Woessner & Kluth, P.A.; Star
Tribune Foundation; the Target Foundation; West Group; and many
individual donors. To you and our many readers across the country,
we send our thanks for your continuing support.

COFFEE HOUSE PRESS books are available to the trade through
our primary distributor, Consortium Book Sales & Distribution,
1045 Westgate Drive, Saint Paul, MN 55114. For personal orders, cata-
logs, or other information, write to: Coffee House Press, 27 North
Fourth Street, Suite 400, Minneapolis, MN 55401.

LIBRARY OF CONGRESS CIP INFORMATION

Major, Clarence.
    Necessary distance : essays and criticism/Clarence Major.—1st ed.
      p. cm.
    ISBN 1-56689-109-4 (alk. paper)
    I. Title.
PS3563.A39 N4 2001
809--DC21

                        00-065894

10 9 8 7 6 5 4 3 2 1
FIRST EDITION

Contents

PART THREE: REVIEWING

PART ONE: VIEWING MYSELF

NECESSARY DISTANCE:
AFTERTHOUGHTS ON BECOMING A WRITER

People have a tendency to ask a writer, *Why* did you become a writer? *How* did you become a writer? Every writer hears such questions over and over. You ever hear anybody ask a butcher a question like that?

So, what's so special about being a writer? Maybe we are simply fascinated by people who are brave (or foolish) enough to go against—and lucky enough to beat—the odds.

We seem fascinated in the same way by the lives of people in show business, and probably for the same reasons the lives of writers interest us.

It is also always amazing to see someone making a living doing something he or she actually enjoys.

I never seriously tried to deal with the questions till I was asked to write my life story. If my autobiography were going to make sense, I thought I'd better try my best to answer both questions.

So, my speaking on the page to you is, in a way, an effort to answer those questions—for myself and possibly for others. I don't expect to succeed, but here goes.

It seems to me that the impulse to write, the *need* to write, is inseparable from one's educational process—which begins at the beginning and never ends.

In some sort of nonobjective way, I can remember being an infant and some of the things I thought about and touched. I had a sister, but my sister didn't have a brother. I had no self because I was *all* self. Gradually, like any developing kid, I shed my self-centered view of the world: saw myself reflected in my mother's eyes, began to perceive the idea of a self. In a way it was at this point that my research as a writer, and as a painter, began. (For me, the two impulses were always inseparable.) The world was a place of magic, and everything I touched was excruciatingly *new.* Without knowing it, my career had begun.

In his meditation on the art of fiction, *Being and Race,* novelist Charles Johnson says: "All art points to others with whom the writer argues about what is. . . . He must have models with which to agree . . . or outright oppose . . . for Nature seems to remain silent. . . ." Reading this passage reminded me of Sherwood Anderson's short story "Death in the Woods," in which the narrator retells the story we are reading because his brother, who told it first, hadn't told it the way it was supposed to be told. In a similar way, that early self of mine had already started its long battle with the history of literature and art.

In the early stages of that battle, some very primary things were going on. By this I mean to say that a writer is usually a person who has to learn how to keep his ego—like his virginity—and lose it at the same time. In other words, he becomes a kind of twin of himself. He remains that self-centered infant while transcending him to become the observer of his own experience and, by extension, the observer of a wide range of experience within his cultural domain. Without any rational self-consciousness at all, early on, my imagination was fed by the need to invent things. My older cousins taught me how to make my own toys—trucks, cars, houses, whole cities. We used old skate wheels for tires. Our parents couldn't afford such luxuries as toys; we were lucky if we got new clothes. Watching physical things like the toys we made take shape, I think, showed me some possibilities. (William Carlos Williams said a poem is like a machine. If I understand what he meant, I can see a connection between what I was making at age seven and poems and stories I tried to write later on.)

Plus the *newness* of everything—trees, plants, the sky—and the need to define everything, on my own terms, was a given. At my grandparents' farm, my cousins and I climbed trees and named the trees we climbed. Painfully, I watched my uncle slaughter hogs and learned about death. I watched my grandmother gather eggs from the chicken nests and learned about birth. I watched her make lye soap and the clothes we wore. But I didn't fully trust the world I was watching. It seemed too full of danger, even while I dared to explore it and attempt to imprint the evidence of my presence upon it—by making things such as toys or drawing pictures in the sand.

Daydreaming as a necessity in the early disposition of a writer is not a new idea. Whether or not it was necessary in my case, I was a guilty practitioner. I say this because I had an almost mystical attachment to nature. If looked at from my parents' point of view, it was not a good sign. I could examine a leaf for hours or spend hours on my knees watching the way ants lived. Behaving like a lazy kid, I followed the flights and landings of birds with spiritual devotion. The frame of mind that put me through those motions was, later, the same frame of mind from which I tried to write a poem or a story: daydreaming, letting it happen, connecting two or three previously unrelated things, making them mean something—together—entirely new. I was hopeless.

And dreams. In dreams I discovered a self going about its business with a mind of its own. I began to watch and to wonder. I was amazed by some of the things I had the nerve to dream about. Sex, for example. Or some wonderful, delicious food! One guilty pleasure after another! This other self often invented these wonderful ways for me to actually get something—even a horse once—that I *knew* I wanted, something no one seriously wanted to give me.

At times, waking up was the hard part. Dream activity was all invention, maybe even the rootbeds of all the conscious, willful invention I wanted to take charge of in the hard indifference of daylight. Unlike the daydreams I spent so much time giving myself to, *these* dreams were not under my control. Later, I started trying to write them down, but I discovered that it was impossible to capture their specific texture. They had to stay where they were. But I tried to imitate them, to make up stories that *sounded* like them. The pattern of these dreams became a model for the imaginative leaps I wanted to make (and couldn't for a long time!) in my poetry and fiction.

My first novel, written at the age of twelve, was twenty pages long. It was the story of a wild, free-spirited horse leading a herd. Influenced by movies, I thought it would make a terrific film, so I sent it to Hollywood. A man named William Self read it and sent it back with a letter of encouragement. I never forgot his kindness. It was the beginning of a long process of learning to live with rejection—not just rejection slips. And that experience too was necessary as a correlation to the writing process, necessary because one of the most important things I was going to have to learn was *how* to detect my own failures and be the first to reject them.

Was there, then, a particular point when I said, *Hey! I'm going to become a writer!* I think there was, but it now seems irrelevant because I must have been evolving toward that conscious moment long, long before I had any idea what was going on. (I was going to have to find my way—with more imperfection than not—through *many* disciplines, such as painting, music, anthropology, history, philosophy, psychology, sociology—before such a consciousness would begin to emerge.)

I think I was in the fifth grade when a girl who sat behind me snuck me a copy of Raymond Radiguet's *Devil in the Flesh.* This was *adult fiction!* And judging from the cover, the book was going to have some good parts. But as it turned out, the *single* good part was the writing itself. I was reading that book one day at home, and about halfway through, I stood up and went crazy with an important discovery: *Writing had a life of its own!* And I soon fell in love with the life of writing, by way of this book—Kay Boyle's translation of Radiguet.

From that moment on, up to about the age of twenty, I set out to discover other books that might challenge my perception forever. Hawthorne's *The Scarlet Letter* showed me how gracefully a story could be told and how terrifying human affairs—and self-deception within those affairs—can be. Conrad's *Heart of Darkness* caught me in an aesthetic network of magic so powerful I never untangled myself. I then went on to read other nineteenth-century, and even earlier works, by Melville, Baudelaire, Emerson, Dostoyevsky, and the like.

But I always hung on with more comfort to the twentieth century. I read J. D. Salinger's *The Catcher in the Rye* early enough for it to have spoken profoundly and directly to me about what I was feeling and thinking about the adult world at the time that its agony affirmed my faith in life. Richard Wright's *Native Son* was an overwhelming experience, and so was Rimbaud's poetry. But the important thing about these discoveries is that each of them led to Cocteau and other French writers, going back to the nineteenth century. Salinger led me to a discovery of modern and contemporary American fiction— Hemingway, Faulkner, Sherwood Anderson, and on and on. Wright led to Dos Passos, to James T. Farrell, to Jean Toomer, to Chester

Himes, to William Gardner Smith, to Ann Petry, to Nella Larsen and other Afro-American writers. Rimbaud led to the discovery of American poetry (which was not so much of a leap as it sounds), to Williams, to Marianne Moore, to Eliot, to cummings. This activity began roughly during the last year of grade school and took on full, focused direction in high school. At the time, none of these writers was being taught in school. I was reading them on my own. In school we had to read O. Henry and Joyce Kilmer.

But during all this time, it was hard to find books that came *alive*. I had to go through hundreds before hitting on the special ones, the ones with the power to shape or reshape perception, to deepen vision, to give me the means to understand myself and other things, to drive away fears and doubts. I found the possibilities of wedding the social and political self to the artistic self in the essays of James Baldwin. Autobiographies such as Billie Holiday's *Lady Sings the Blues* and Mezz Mezzrow's *Really the Blues* were profound reading experiences. These books, and books like them, taught me that even life, with more pain than one individual had any right to, was still worth spending some time trying to get through—and, like Billie's and Mezz's, with dignity and inventiveness.

Although I was learning to appreciate good writing, I had no command of the language myself. I had the *need* to write well, but that was about all. Only the most sensitive teacher—and there were two or three along the way—was able to detect some talent and imagination in my efforts. Every time I gathered enough courage to dream of writing seriously, the notion ended in frustration, or sometimes despair. Not only did I not have command of the language, I didn't have the necessary distance on experience to have anything important to say about even the things I knew something about.

I daydreamed about a solution to these problems: I could learn to write and go out and live it up in order to have experience. But this solution would take time, and I was not willing to wait for time. In my sense of urgency, I didn't have that much time.

Meanwhile, there were a few adults I ventured to show my efforts to. One teacher told me I couldn't possibly have written the story I showed her. It was *too good*—which meant that it was a hell of a lot better than I had thought. But rather than gaining more self-confidence, the experience became grounds for the loss of respect for her intelligence. Among the other adults who saw my early works was my mother, who encouraged me as much as her understanding permitted, and a young, college-educated man who was a friend of the family's. He told me I was pretty good.

I was growing up in Chicago, and my life therefore had a particular social shape. The realities I was discovering in books didn't, at first, seem to correspond to the reality around me. At the time, I didn't have enough distance to see the connections.

The fact is, the writerly disposition that was then evolving was shaped by my life in Chicago—in the classroom and on the playground—as well as it was being shaped during the times I spent alone with books, and anywhere else for that matter. Which is only one way of saying that a writer doesn't make most of his or her own decisions about personal vision or outlook.

Jean Paul Sartre in *What Is Literature?* makes the observation that Richard Wright's destiny as a writer was chosen for him by the circumstances of birth and social history. One can go even further and say that it's as difficult to draw the line between where a sensibility is influenced by the world around it and where it is asserting its own presence in that world as it is to say whether or not essence precedes existence.

To put it another way, the educational process against which my would-be writerly disposition was taking formation was political. Political because I quickly had to learn how to survive, for example on the playground. It was not easy since I had an instinctive dislike for violence. But the playground was a place where the dramas of life were acted out. Radiguet's book (and Jean Paul Rossi's *Awakening,* too) had, to some extent, dealt with the same territory. As a microcosm of life, it was no doubt one of the first social locations in which I was forced to observe some of the ways people relate—or don't relate—to each other. Among a number of things, I learned how to survive the pecking order rituals with my wits rather than my fists. This was an area where books and art could not save me. But later on, I was going to see how what I *had* to learn in self-defense carried over to the creative effort.

The classroom, too, was not a place where one wanted to let one's guard down for too long. To be liked and singled out by a teacher often meant getting smashed in the mouth or kicked in the stomach on the playground. If one demonstrated intelligence in school, one could almost certainly expect to hear about it later on the way home. It was simply not cool for boys to be smart in class. A smart boy was a sissy and deserved to get his butt kicked.

I had to be very quiet about my plans to become a writer. I couldn't talk with friends about what I read. I mean, why wasn't I out playing basketball?

All of this, in terms of education (or plans to become a writer) meant that if you wanted to learn anything (or try to write something, for example), you had to do it without *flaunting* what you were doing. Naturally some smart but less willful kids gave in, in the interest of survival; they learned how to fail in order to live in the safety zone of the majority. And for those of us who didn't want to give in, it was hard to keep how well we were doing a secret because the teacher would tell the class who got the best grades.

I was also facing another crisis. If I wanted to write, eventually I had to face an even larger problem—publication. I thought that if I were ever lucky enough to get anything published, say in a school magazine or newspaper, it would be a success I would have to keep quiet about among most of my friends, and certainly around those out to put me in my place. And God forbid that my first published work should be a poem. Only sissies wrote poetry.

But I couldn't go on like that. I remember once breaking down and saying to hell with it. I walked around the school building with a notebook writing down everything I saw, trying to translate the life around me, minute by minute, into words. I must have filled twenty pages with very boring descriptions. A girl I liked, but didn't have the nerve to talk to, saw me. She thought I was doing homework. When I told her what I was up to, she gave me this strange, big-eyed look, then quickly disappeared—forever—from my life.

I now realize that I must have been a difficult student for teachers to understand. At times I was sort of smart, at other times I left a lot to be desired. One teacher thought I might be retarded, another called me a genius. Not knowing what else to do with me, the administrators, in frustration, appointed me art director of the whole school of 8,000 students, during my last year.

Why art director? Actually my first passion was for painted pictures rather than the realities I discovered in books. Before my first clear memories I was drawing and painting, while the writing started at a time within memory. So, I think it is important (in the context of "how" and "why," where the writing is concerned) to try to understand what this visual experience has meant for me.

At about the age of twelve, I started taking private art lessons from a South Side painter, Gus Nall. I even won a few prizes. So, confidence in an ability to visually express myself came first. But what I learned from painting, I think, carried over into my writing from the beginning.

My first articulate passion was for the works of Vincent van Gogh. This passion started with a big show of his work that the Art Institute of Chicago hung in the early fifties. There were about a hundred and fifty pieces.

I pushed my way through the crowded galleries, stunned every step of the way. I kept going back. I was not sophisticated enough to know how to articulate for myself what these things were doing to me, but I knew I was profoundly moved. So on some level, I no doubt did sense the power of the painterliness of those pictures of winding country paths, working peasants, flower gardens, rooftops, the stillness of a summer day. They really got to me.

Something in me went out to the energy of Vincent's "Sunflowers," for example. I saw him as one who broke the rules and transcended. Where I came from, no socially well-behaved person ever went out and gathered sunflowers for a vase in the home. No self-respecting grown man spent ten years painting pictures he couldn't sell. On the South Side of Chicago, everything of value had a price tag.

Vincent, then, was at least one important model for my rebellion. The world I grew up in told me that the only proper goals were to make money, get an education, become a productive member of society, go to church, and have a family—pretty much in that order. But I had found my alternative models, and it was too late for that world to get its hooks in me. I wasn't planning to do anything less than the greatest thing I could think of: I wanted to be like van Gogh, like Richard Wright, like Jean Toomer, like Rimbaud, like Bud Powell.

In the meantime, I went home from the van Gogh exhibition and tried to create the same effects from the life around me. I drew my stepfather soaking his feet in a pan of water, my older sister braiding my younger sister's hair, the bleak view of rooftops from my bedroom window, my mother in bed sick, anything that struck me as compositionally viable. In this rather haphazard way, I was learning to *see*. I suspect there was a certain music and innocence in Vincent's lines and colors that gave me a foundation for my own attempts at *representing*—first through drawing and painting, and very soon after in the poetry I was writing. The first poems I tried to write were strongly imagistic, in the Symbolist tradition.

I made thousands of sketches of these sorts of everyday things. I was responding to the things of my world. I had already lived in two or three different worlds: in a southern city (Atlanta); in a rural country setting; and now in Chicago, an urban, brutal, stark setting. We moved a lot—so much so that my sense of place was always changing. Home was where we happened to be. Given this situation, I think the fact that Vincent felt like an alien in his own land (and was actually an alien in France), and that this sense of estrangement carried over emotionally into his work found a strong correlating response in me.

If there were disadvantages in being out of step, there were just as many advantages. I was beginning to engage myself passionately in painting and writing, and this passion would carry me through a lot of difficulties and disappointments simply because I *had* it. I saw many people with no strong interest in *anything*. Too many of them perished for lack of a dream long before I thought possible.

At fourteen, this passionate need to create (and apparently the need to *share* it, too) caused me to try to go public, despite the fact that I knew I was doing something eccentric. One of my uncles ran a printing shop. I gathered enough confidence in my poetry to pay him ten dollars to print fifty copies of a little booklet of my own poetry. The poems reflect the influence of Rimbaud, van Gogh, and Impressionism generally—even used French words I didn't understand.

Once I had the books in hand, I realized that I didn't know more than three people who might be interested in seeing a copy. I gave one to one of my English teachers. I gave my mother three copies. I gave my best poet friend a copy. I may have also given my art teacher, Mr.

Fouche, a copy. And the rest of the edition was stored in a closet. They stayed there till, by chance, a year or two later I discovered how bad the poems were and destroyed the remaining copies.

Shortly after the van Gogh exhibition, the Institute sponsored a large showing of the works of Paul Cézanne, whose work I knew a bit from the few pieces in the permanent collection. I went to the exhibition not so much because I was attracted to Cézanne but because it was there—and I felt that I should appreciate Cézanne. At fifteen that was not easy. And the reasons I found it difficult to appreciate Cézanne as much as I thought I should had to do with, I later learned, my inability to understand at a gut level what he was about, what his *intentions* were. Cézanne's figures looked stiff and ill-proportioned. His landscapes, like his still lifes, seemed made of stone or wood or metal. Everything in Cézanne was unbending, lifeless.

I looked at the apples and oranges on the table and understood their *weight* and how important the *sense* of that weight was in understanding Cézanne's intentions. I wanted to say, yes, it's a great accomplishment. But why couldn't I *like it?* I was not yet sophisticated enough to realize that all great art—to the unsophisticated viewer—at first appears *ugly,* even repulsive. And I had yet to discover Gertrude Stein in any serious way, to discover her attempts to do with words what Cézanne was doing with lines and color.

It took many years to acquire an appreciation for Cézanne, but doing so, in its way, was as important to my development as a writer as was my passion for van Gogh. But the appreciation started, in its troubled way, with that big show. When I finally saw the working out of the *sculpturing* of a created reality (to paraphrase James Joyce), I experienced a breakthrough. Cézanne appealed to my rational side. I began going to Cézanne for a knowledge of the inner, mechanical foundation of art, and for an example of a self-conscious exploration of composition. All of this effort slowly taught me how to *see* the significant aspects of writing and how they correspond to those in painting. Discovering how perspective corresponded to point of view was a real high point.

These two painters, van Gogh and Cézanne, were catalysts for me, but there were other painters important for similar reasons: Toulouse-Lautrec, Degas, Bonnard, Cassatt, and Munch, for the way they intensely scrutinized private and public moments; Edward Hopper for his ability to invest a view of a house or the interior of a room with a profound sense of mortality; Matisse for his play, his rhythm, his design. I was attracted by the intimacy of subject matter in their work.

I also had very strong responses to Gauguin. He excited and worried me at the same time. At first, I was suspicious of a European seeking purity among dark people. (I placed D. H. Lawrence in the same category.) Later, I realized Gauguin's story was more complex than that (as was Lawrence's). But more important to me was the fact that Gauguin's paintings used flat, blunt areas of vivid colors. Their sumptuousness drew a profoundly romantic response from me. Not only did I try to paint that way for a period, I also thought I saw the possibility of creating simple, flat images with simple sentences or lines.

For a while I was especially attracted to painters who used paint thickly. Turner's seascapes were incredible. Up close they looked abstract. Utrillo's scenes of Paris, Rouault's bumpy people, Albert Ryder's horrible dreams, Kokoschka's profusion of layered effects— these rekindled feelings that had started with van Gogh. (Years later, I came to appreciate Beckman and Schiele for similar reasons.) To paint that way—expressively, and apparently fast—had a certain appeal. It was just a theory, but worth playing with; in correlation, it might be possible to make words move with that kind of self-apparent urgency, that kind of reflexive brilliance. The expressionistic writers— Lawrence, Mansfield, Joyce, and others—had done it.

I kept moving from one fascination to another. Later, the opposite approach attracted me. The lightness of Picasso's touch was as remarkable as a pelican in flight. If I could make a painting or poem move like that—like the naturalness of walking or sleeping—I would be lucky.

I was easily seduced. I got lost in the dreams of Chagall, in the summer laziness of Monet, in the waves of Winslow Homer, in the blood and passion of Orozco, in the bright, simple designs of Rivera, in the fury of Jackson Pollock, in the struggle of de Kooning, in the selflessness of Vermeer, in the light and shadow of Rembrandt, in the plushness of Rubens, in the fantastic mystery of Bosch, in the power of Michelangelo and Tintoretto, in the incredible sensitivity and intelligence of Leonardo da Vinci, in the earthly dramas of Daumier and Millet. Later on, when I discovered Afro-American art, I got equally caught up in the works of Jacob Lawrence, Archibald Motley, Henry Tanner, Edward Bannister, and others. I was troubled from the beginning by the absence of Afro-American painters, novelists, and poets, generally, whom I might have turned to as models. I was seventeen before, on my own, I discovered the *reason* they were absent: The system had hidden them. It was that simple. They had existed since the beginning but were, for well-known reasons, made officially nonexistent.

Although this learning process was a slow and very long one, and I wasn't always conscious of even the things I successfully managed to transfer into my own painting and writing, I can now look back and realize that I must always have been more fascinated by technique than I was by subject matter. The subject of a novel or a painting seemed irrelevant: a nude, a beach scene, a stand of trees, a story of an army officer and a seventeen-year-old girl in a foreign country, a lyrical view of a horrible accident. It didn't matter! What did matter was *how* the painter or storyteller or poet seduced me into the story, into the picture, into the poem.

I guess I also felt the need to submerge myself in the intellectual excitement of an artistic community, but I couldn't find one. Just about every writer I'd ever heard of seemed to have had such nourishment: Hemingway, Stein, and Fitzgerald in Paris among the other expatriates. . . . But I was not in touch with any sort of exciting literary or artistic life (outside of visits to the Institute) on the South Side. True, I had met a couple of writers—Willard Motley and Frank London Brown—and a few painters—Gus Nall, Archibald Motley, and a couple of others. But I felt pretty isolated. Plus these people were a lot older and didn't seem to have much time to spare. So, I clumsily started my own little magazine—a thing called *Coercion Review.* It became my substitute for an artistic community and, as such, a means of connecting (across the country and even across the ocean) with a larger, cultural world—especially with other writers and poets.

I published the works of writers I corresponded with, and they published mine; in a way, this became our way of *workshopping,* as my students say, our manuscripts. When we found something acceptable, it meant (or so we thought) that the particular piece had succeeded. We were wrong more often than not. It was an expensive way to learn what *not* to publish, and how to live with what couldn't be unpublished.

Seeing my work in print increased my awareness of the many problems I still faced in my writing at, say, the age of eighteen. I wrote to William Carlos Williams for help. I also wrote to Langston Hughes. They were generous. (In fact, Williams not only criticized the poetry but told me of his feelings of despair as a poet.)

Rushing into print was teaching me that I not only needed distance on approach (the selection of point of view, for example) and subject matter *before* starting a work, but I also needed to slow down, to let a manuscript wait, to see if it could stand up under my own developing ability to edit during future readings, when my head would be clear of manuscript birth fumes. As a result, my awareness of what I was doing, of its aesthetic value, increased. I became more selective about what I sent out.

During all this time, I was also listening to music. Critics of Afro-American writing often find reason to compare black writing to black music. Each of my novels, at one time or another, has been compared to either blues songs or jazz compositions. I've never doubted that critics had a right to do this. But what was I to make of the fact that I had also grown up with Tin Pan Alley, bluegrass, *and* European classical music? I loved Chopin and Beethoven.

Something was wrong. It seemed to me that Jack Kerouac, for example, had gotten as many jazz motifs into his work as James Baldwin. At a certain point, when I noticed that critics were beginning to see rhythms of music as a basis for my lines or sentences, to say nothing of content, I backed up and took a closer look. I had to argue, at least with myself, that all of the music I'd loved while growing up found its aesthetic way into my writing—or none of it did.

True, I had been overwhelmingly caught up in the bebop music of Bud Powell when I was a kid—I loved "Un Poco Loco," thought it was the most inventive piece of music I had ever heard, loved all of his original compositions ("Hallucinations," "I Remember Clifford," "Oblivion," "Glass Enclosure," and on and on—and as I said before, I swore by the example of his devotion to his art).

But I soon moved on out, in a natural way, from Powell into an appreciation of the progressive music of other innovators, such as

Thelonius Monk, Lester Young, Sonny Stitt, John Coltrane, Clifford Brown, Miles Davis, Dizzy Gillespie, Charlie Parker, Dexter Gordon, and Ornette Coleman—and, at the same time, I was discovering Jimmy Rushing, Bessie Smith, Billie Holiday, Joe Turner, Dinah Washington—singers from my father's generation and before.

My feeling, on this score, is that Afro-American music generally (along with other types of music I grew up hearing) had a pervasive cultural importance for me. I think I need to take this assumption into consideration in trying to trace in myself the shape of what I hope has become some sort of sensitivity not only to music but also to poetry, fiction, painting, and the other arts. I've already mentioned the importance of other disciplines—anthropology, history, philosophy, psychology, sociology—in an attempt to lay some sort of intellectual foundation from which to write. Without going through the long, hopelessly confusing tangle of my own profoundly troubled questing, I think I can sum up what I came away with (as it relates to themes I chose or the themes that chose me) in pretty simple terms.

I remember my excitement when I began to understand cultural patterns. Understanding the nature of kinship—family, clan, tribe—gave me insight into relationships in the context of my own family, community, and country. I was also fascinated to discover, while reading about tribal people, something called a caste system. I immediately realized that I had grown up in communities, both in the South and the North, where one kind of caste system or another was practiced. Being extremely light or extremely dark, for example, often meant penalization by the community.

Totem practices also fascinated me because I was able to turn from books and see examples in everyday life: There were people who wore good-luck charms and fetishes such as rabbits' feet on keychains. I became aware, in deeper ways, of the significance of ritual and ceremony, and how to recognize examples when I saw them. It was a breakthrough for me to begin to understand *how* cultures (my own included) rationalized their own behavior.

The formation of myths—stories designed to explain why things were as they were—was of deep interest to me. Myths, I discovered, governed the behavior and customs I saw every day, customs concerning matters of birth, death, parents, grandparents, marriage, grief, luck, dances, husband-and-wife relationships, siblings, revenge, joking, adoption, sexual relations, murder, fights, food, toilet training, game playing. You name it.

Reading Freud, and other specialists of the mind, I thought would help me understand better how to make characters more convincing. At the same time I hoped to get a better insight into myself—which in the long run would also improve my writing. I read Freud's little study of Leonardo da Vinci. I was also interested in gaining a better understanding of the nature of creativity itself.

But even more than that, I was interested in the religious experiences psychologists wrote about. I consciously sought ways to understand religious frenzy and faith in rational terms. I was beginning to think how, as too much nationalism tends to lead to fascism, too much blind religion could be bad for one's mental health. To me, the human mind and the human heart began to look like very, very dangerously nebulous things. But at the same time, I kept on trying to accept the world and its institutions at face value, to understand them on their own terms. After all, who was I to come along and seriously question *everything?* The degree to which I did question was more from innocence than from arrogance.

I was actually optimistic because I thought knowledge might lead me somewhere refreshing, might relieve the burden of ignorance. If I could only understand schizophrenia or hysteria, mass brainwashing and charisma, paganism, asceticism, brotherly love. Why did some individuals feel called to preach and others feel overwhelmed with galloping demons? What was the function of dreaming? I skimmed the Kinsey reports and considered monastic life. I read Alan Watts and was a Buddhist for exactly one week.

I liked the gentle way Reich criticized Freud and, in the process, chiseled out his own psychoanalytical principles. If I ever thought psychoanalysis could help me personally, I was not mad enough to think I could afford it. I did notice, though, how writers of fiction, and poets too, from around the turn of the century on, were using the principles of psychoanalysis as a tool for exploring behavior in fiction and poetry. So I gave it a shot. But the real challenge, I soon learned, was to find a way to absorb some of this stuff and at the same time keep the evidence of it out of my own writing.

Yet I kept hoping for some better, more suitable approach to human experience. If a better one existed, I had no idea. But there wasn't much to hold on to in psychoanalysis or psychology, and even less in sociology, where I soon discovered that statistics could be made to prove anything the researcher wanted to prove. If the *very presence* of the researcher were itself a contamination, what hope was there for this thing everybody called objectivity?

While I was able to make these connections between theory and reality, I was still seeking answers to questions I had asked since the beginning—*Who and what am I?* Questions we discover later in life are not so important. Everywhere I turned—to philosophy, to psychology—I was turned back upon myself and left with more questions than I had at the start.

Growing up in America when I did, while aiming to be a writer, was a disturbing experience. (Every generation is sure it is more disturbed than the previous one and less lucky than the forthcoming one.) This troublesome feeling was real, though; it wasn't just growing pains. There was something else, and I knew it. And I finally found part of the explanation. My sense of myself was hampered by my country's sense of itself. My country held an idealistic image of itself that was, in many aspects of its life, vastly different from its actual, unvarnished self. There was severe poverty, ignorance, disease, corruption, racism, sexism, and there was war—all too often undeclared.

But I, as a writer, could not afford the luxury of a vision of my own experience as sentimental as the one suggested by my country (of itself, of me). As I grew up, I was trying to learn how to see through the superficial, and to touch, in my writing, the essence of experience—in all of its possible wonderment, agony, or glory.

Despite the impossibility of complete success, I continue.

I want to be as forthright as possible with these afterthoughts because I know that afterthoughts can never *truly* recapture the moments they try to touch back upon. Each moment, it seems to me, in which a thought occurs, has more to do with that moment itself than with anything in the past. This, to my way of thinking, turns out to be more positive than negative, because it supports the continuous nature of life, and that of art, too. The creative memory, given expression, is no enemy of the past, nor does its self-focus diminish its authority.

DISCOVERING WALT WHITMAN

I first found the work of Walt Whitman when I was seventeen years
old, in a bleak Catholic Salvage Store on Forty-first Street near
State, in segregated Chicago. The copy of *Leaves of Grass* was very old,
very musty, but the price was only twenty-five cents. I bought the
book and lived with it for quite a while, despite its odor. (My books,
in general, were a weird assortment, many of them having come from
such dusty shops on the South Side.)

I often lay in my bed in my small room in our home and fingered
the old book. I frequently wondered about it having been published
during Whitman's lifetime. How remote was the possibility that his
hands had touched it? Whitman had died sixty-two years before that
year in the summer of my growing pains, yet the physical reality of
that book gave me a sense of him different from the one that came so
forcefully through his lines. Witness:

> *I loafe and invite my soul,*
> *I lean and loafe at my ease, observing a spear of summer grass.*

(from "Song of Myself")

What else, except this, is meant by the attainment of oneness with all
that is?

And how well, from my childhood's brief stay in the forest
behind my grandmother's home, I knew what Whitman meant in the
unrestrained glory concealed in the leanness of lines such as,

With delicate-colored blossoms,
    and heart-shaped leaves of rich green
A sprig, with its flower, I
    break.

(from "Song of Myself")

But there was never any Whitman in school. There was Shakespeare. Whitman was too revolutionary for South Side high schools.

Still, I was always discovering things on my own. Just as I had discovered Paul Laurence Dunbar and Phillis Wheatley, I found Whitman, and enjoyed his openness, his emotional outbursts, his long lines measured against short lines, his healthy frankness in matters sexual and racial, his acceptance of his own body without the usual Puritan hangups, his natural understanding of who and what human beings are, what they amount to, living together in a society. Whitman fought social restrictions, the Puritanical stifling air. But it is still here to breathe.

Whitman is valuable because he was a good and original poet and because he found his own way to be good at making poems. I remember sitting on the floor in the library on an Air Force base in Cheyenne, Wyoming for two hours one day when it was below zero outside, reading and rereading *Leaves.* It kept coming back into my life. And even now, while describing important events in my life, Whitman has a place again.

William Carlos Williams (who read some of my early poems and wrote to me about them), in *Spring and All,* said: "When in the condition of imaginative suspense only will the writing have reality, as explained partially in what precedes—Not to attempt, at that time, to set values on the word being used, according to pre-supposed measures, but to write down that which happens at that time—"

When I was working on the *Dictionary of Afro-American Slang,* I discovered that Whitman had a message for me: "Language," he wrote, "is not an abstract construction of the learned, or of dictionary-makers, but is something arising out of the work, needs, ties, joys, affections, tastes, of long generations of humanity, and has its basis broad and low, close to the ground."

And the "ground" to Whitman, never forget, was not the symbol of degradation. It stood for all glory.

A PARIS FANTASY TRANSFORMED

Paris! Why Paris? Why did I—or any African American artist or writer—go to Paris?

When I was a teenager in the 1950s, African American artists (and writers, dancers, jazz musicians, actors) had already enjoyed a long relationship with Paris. Even before the end of slavery, free mulattos, some of them artists, were traveling to Paris and other parts of Europe. They went for many different reasons. One of the best known of those who went in the nineteenth century was the painter Henry O. Tanner.

In retrospect, I realize that my motives for going to Paris were similar to those of the people who had gone before me. Although they had various personal reasons for settling in Paris, there was a commonality about their motives. Beauford Delaney, for example, in 1951, stopped in Paris on his way to Rome, found there the artistic nourishment he needed, and stayed.

As a young man, I read Richard Wright and James Baldwin, and knew they lived in Paris. Baldwin, who was a good friend of Delaney's, said African Americans went to Paris because: "We . . . had presumably put down all formulas and all safety in favor of the chilling unpredictability of experience."

Considering this history, I can now see how I, as a teenager, got focused on a fantasy of Paris as a desirable place to live, paint, and write. I had been lucky enough to win a scholarship to attend James Nelson Raymond's lecture and sketch classes at the Art Institute of Chicago, where, by the way, I spent a lot of time in front of Tanner's "Two Disciples at the Tomb," gazing at the dramatic light on the faces of Peter and John. At the Institute, my earliest fantasies of Paris fed on scenes of the city by French painters—especially those of Maurice Utrillo's, his views of Montmartre. Paris was the place of so much that interested me. Art! Poetry! Philosophy! I remember at age seventeen struggling through a book by Sartre on Existentialism, understanding perhaps only about twenty percent of it.

The presence of Paris was also surprisingly vivid on the South Side of Chicago while I was growing up. The painter Archibald Motley was back from Paris, living in Chicago. We both had paintings in Gayles Gallery on Sixty-third. I admired his cool, gray Paris cafe and street life paintings. Ex-Parisian jazz singer Lil Armstrong (Louis's first wife) held a kind of Chicago salon for young artists like myself. Regularly I also saw Ollie Harrington's funny, humane "Bootsie" cartoons in the black newspapers, sent over from Paris, where he lived. And Josephine Baker used to come over to our neighborhood in Chicago and dance for us on the stage of the Regal Theater at Forty-seventh and South Parkway. She brought with her what I imagined was the glamour of Paris.

But the Paris I fantasized about most often was a Paris of grimy bistros, Toulouse-Lautrec-type dance halls, narrow dark streets, dimly lighted bars in Montmartre, small dusty bookshops, the rue des Lombards, the rue Blomet—a nocturnal Paris, a place of outcasts, poets, and artists. Orwell's *Down and Out in Paris and London* gave me a vivid picture of the "solitary half-mad grooves of life" lived in these areas. This was, in a sense, also Henry Miller's postwar Paris.

Definitely not Hemingway's young man "lucky enough to have lived in Paris" before a certain age, and therefore able to carry always in my bosom "a moveable feast," I didn't get around to going to Paris till I was thirty-five. By then I had somehow become more visible as a novelist and poet than as a painter, though I was still painting persistently. But on this first trip there, caught up in the endless tourist rounds, my fantasy-Paris was nowhere in sight. My frustration was almost enough to cause me to agree with Virginia Woolf when she wrote, "Paris is a hostile brilliant city."

But subsequent trips showed me Paris was no more hostile than any other big city, and considerably more brilliant—and beautiful—

as can be seen, for example, in Delaney's street scenes. His impasto technique, whirling expressionistic lines, called to mind van Gogh and the Fauves. I'll never forget a day in 1982, in the South of France in Jimmy Baldwin's home, when I found myself in a room full of Delaney canvases.

Although I also lived and taught, for a year and a half, at the University of Nice (near Jimmy's home), it was in Paris, with all the various trips stitched together as a kind of tapestry, that the real artistic nourishment happened. Because I paint, Paris was a special, symbolic place for me. But as a writer, I found just as much inspiration there.

Paris provided me with some of the same aesthetic energy and freedom that it had always given artists. I went there again and again to connect with that energy. A city that named its streets after artists and writers, not politicians, was my kind of city. A city that had so many art museums and galleries that art seemed part of daily life, in my book, was not an exotic city but a sensible one.

Yet how was I personally rewarded and changed by this real Paris sojourn? While staying in various parts of the city during the eighties, and for an extended period in 1985 in the 11th Arrondissement, near Pere-Lachaise Cemetery, I came to make a Paris of my own. We Americans were getting seven francs to the dollar, so my wife Pamela and I felt we could splurge occasionally, but there were always free things just as good to do. Walking through the cemetery and reading the headstones was a chance to touch many who had fed my earlier fantasies—Seurat, Modigliani, Gertrude Stein, Richard Wright himself.

Seeing the difference between my American culture and the French helped reveal who I had been and who I was now becoming. Paradoxically, Paris gave me my national identity, although I hadn't gone there looking for that part of myself.

To be sure, there was as much racism in France as in the States, but in Paris, I was not the target of French racism. As soon as the French discovered I was not an African or Arab from one of their former colonies, I was treated well. This was an ironic and ambiguous position to be in.

All my life, in my own country, I had seen Americans treat Africans and Arabs—people they had no historical ties to—with the same kind of dubious respect. Despite its questionable basis, it was better

treatment than black Americans got. The point is, in Paris—as pathetic as it sounds—I *felt American* for the first time, and in a way I had
never felt at home.

Plus Pamela and I found that Parisian life itself—in the way we
lived our day-to-day life—was sensible and satisfying. We came to
know the neighborhood shopkeepers and vendors, and they us. Like
those before us, we had our favorite cafes in our own neighborhood,
and the waiters, after a time, didn't need to be told what to bring to
the table. I would amuse Pamela by making up stories about other
customers or passers-by. In my sketch book, I'd jot down the outline
of an interesting face, or try to capture the motion of an interesting
man or woman walking by. In one such cafe, off Place de La Reunion,
we could sit for hours watching the cat in the window watching the
people walking by, or sit in the park across the street and watch the
children play. This Paris was far from that grimy rue Blomet Paris, or
the dark, mysterious rue des Lombards of my fantasy. It was closer to
Renoir's or Degas's Paris.

Venturing beyond the neighborhood, we of course always ran
into tourists. Because of them, galleries and museums tended to be
crowded. One night, Pamela came up with a plan to get around the
problem. The next morning we rushed off to the Jeu de Paume to be
at the front of the line. When the doors opened, instead of doing the
first floor with the mob, we shot directly upstairs and had all the great
van Goghs to ourselves for almost an hour. Our skipping the first floor
confused the guards, and for awhile they watched us closely, obviously
on the lookout for any further false moves on our part. When the mob
hit the second floor, we were ready to go.

The last time Pamela and I were in Paris, one of the first things
we did on our last full day was to go for a walk along Quai de Gesvres.
It was one of those clear spring mornings that, in itself, makes you
happy. We could see Notre-Dame. A tourist boat was moving slowly
down river toward the port at Hotel de Ville. From the boat people
waved, and we waved back.

But, despite the precariousness of my status as a foreigner, I felt consistently good about being in Paris. And I understood what Elizabeth
Barrett Browning felt while on her honeymoon there, when she wrote
to a friend that she and Robert "were satisfied with the *idea* of Paris."

I was invited to Yugoslavia because Galway Kinnell once gave my name, by mail, to Meto Jovanovski in Yugoslavia. Meto was planning to translate American poetry for a Macedonian anthology. This was in October 1973 when Galway and I were teaching at Sarah Lawrence. Meto recommended that Yugoslavia's International Poetry Festival invite me as the official United States representative. I was first invited in 1974 but was unable to accept the invitation. During the spring of 1975 while I was participating in the visiting writer's program at Columbia University, William Jay Smith, its acting director, told me about his trip to Yugoslavia for the festival in 1974. His description excited my imagination. At the same time an invitation to participate in the 1975 Yugoslavian festival arrived. Traveling expenses would cost way over a thousand dollars. The festival would handle expenses while I was there, but the problem was how to pay for transportation. Bill Smith contacted some people he knew in the State Department, and thereby sparked the interest that finally caused the U.S. government to sponsor my trip. Technically this was called a cultural grant.

Someone suggested that, during a time when President Leopold Sedar Senghor of Senegal was to receive an important literary prize at the festival, it would be politically hip for the United States to have a black poet there. I don't know the motives of the State Department, but I do think I know the motives of the Yugoslavs: they were not racial.

The first official meeting of the participants took place at eleven the next morning at the Bristol Hotel, about twenty minutes by bus from the Metropol. The Bristol was in Struga. Gathered around a table in the meeting room were Meteja Matevski, the festival's president, several vice presidents, and the director, Jovan Strezovski. The meeting was brief: a few words of welcome, some hints as to what was to come, some theory.

Then we all went out on the terrace for lunch.

Here, in a relaxed atmosphere, we began to meet people. Herbert Kuhner, an American, introduced himself. Kuhner lived in Austria and said he supported himself by doing translations. He also said he was a poet and fiction writer who had attended many of these festivals. I ordered a bottle of good Holland beer and my wife Sharyn had coffee. One of Senghor's press agents joined us. He had lived in the United States for some years and we exchanged a few impressions. Very soon we were talking with a wide variety of poets: Fatty Said, from Egypt, who reminded me in manner and appearance of Calvin Hernton, from America; tall, handsome, quiet Saadi Yousif, from Iraq, who also wrote short stories; E. M. de Melo Castro, a friendly, bearded, and plump young man from Portugal, one of Portugal's leading young poets; Waldo Leyva Portal, from Cuba; Lassi Nummi and his wife from Finland; Hans van de Waarsenburg from the Netherlands, with a head of long, silky blond hair and a thick beard. His girlfriend or wife, Riet, was with him; she was beautiful; there was the big Viking, Kjell-Erik Vindtorn, from Norway; and Frank De Crits and Eddy von Vliet, both of Belgium; Sergio Macias, originally from Chile, was presently from the Instituto Latinoamerica in Rostock; Homero Aridjis, with his warm smile, originally from Mexico, was presently from the Hague where he was serving as cultural attaché in the Mexican Embassy.

After supper at the Metropol, we all went to the official opening of the festival at the House of Poetry in Struga. The ritual lighting of the festival fires in front of the building had already taken place earlier in the day.

Our books were carefully displayed in the exhibition hall. Hundreds stood inspecting them. Guards watched to make sure no one touched. We could inspect the covers of books by Castro Nummi, Vendtorn, Macias, Vliet, De Crits, Waarsenburg, Portal, Yousif, and Fatty Said. If a guard happened to turn his back, of course we got a brief chance to open them. Senghor's books occupied the center of the exhibition. His press agents were there already though President Senghor himself was still in Belgrade talking politics with President

Tito. Senghor would arrive tomorrow afternoon. This whole affair, the entire festival, was in honor and memory of the Yugoslav poet Ivo Andrić, a Nobel Prize winner.

From the *English* program notes we knew vaguely what was happening: Jovan Strezovski made the introductory remarks, opening the ceremony; then the readings; then, the language of all people—a concert performed by the Macedonian Philharmonic Orchestra conducted by Pero Petrovski.

Scene: next morning, Bistrol Hotel. I'm in the Symposium Room listening to speeches translated through earphones. Sharyn is doing the same thing next to me. Young Yugoslav poet Tomaž Šalamun comes in. He reminds me that I've promised him I'd allow him to interview me before the television camera for Television Skopje. I excuse myself and Tomaž and I go out to the terrace where they have the camera all set. For twenty minutes we discuss poetry, fiction, form, technique, language.

After the morning symposium, Sharyn and I sat on the patio under a bright canopy talking with one of Senghor's press secretaries. The radio and television people were still busy interviewing various foreign visitors. The lake was calm and light blue, with long streaks of yellow light rippling across it. Above, in an otherwise clear sky, a few clouds drifted out toward the distant mountains of Albania. A Macedonian newspaper reporter introduced himself, and with Sharyn's help, speaking French, asked me a few questions about my work and American literature in general. (The next morning we discovered I was grossly misquoted—made to say many contradictory things that supported the reporter's political views of America.)

Later. Outside the House of Poetry, Sharyn and I were catching fresh air, night air. Inside, Yugoslavs were still reading and reciting their poems. We'd already listened to over an hour's worth of it. Presently, we saw Kjell-Erik approaching us. He too felt restless, so the three of us went along the river walkway, rubbing shoulders with hundreds of people out for a night stroll; at the bridge we crossed and went down the other side till we came to an outdoor cafe. We took a table and ordered beer. Sharyn had campari. Kjell-Erik was telling us of his adventures in New Orleans, where he once stopped while working a fishing boat, when Homero, Eddy von Vliet, and Frank joined us. In a somewhat smug manner we talked about the shortcomings of the present festival, its lack of effective organization, then, perhaps feeling guilty, we outlined its virtues, even mentioning how valuable its lack of organization was in the long run.

This was also the night I met Meto Jovanovski for the first time. He reminded me that he and I had corresponded, and that Galway Kinnell had put us in touch with each other. Meto was brought over to us by two American college students, Paul and Nelljean. Both were aspiring poets working on MFAs at a university in one of the Southern states.

Later that night, on what was officially called "Night Without Punctuation," there was a party for the participants at the Bristol's cafe. This was the 29th. After a vegetarian dinner, Sharyn and I joined friends at one of the crowded tables near the stage, where a local band was making loud, brassy music. Already seated at the table were Hans and Riet, Homero, Frank, Eddy, and Kjell-Erik. We all watched Kjell-Erik line up about seven tiny glasses of very sweet wine and drink them all without stopping. I ordered dry white wine and turned to watch the people on the floor, who had begun to dance holding hands and forming a long line, moving snakelike between the tables. They were singing and jumping about awkwardly and having a lot of fun. An African poet went up to the microphone and recited a powerfully revolutionary poem full of chants and barks, and everybody cheered and laughed which was not the right response, but then the poem was also wrong for the occasion, but it didn't matter. A woman from Belgium, a well-known poet, kept coming over to our table, pulling at my arm trying to get me to go up and read one of my poems. To demonstrate how easy it was, she took the microphone and yelled one of her own poems into it, and people screamed with joy. Then somebody else read a slow poem and nobody paid any attention. Then Homero decided to do it and nobody noticed or listened, and when he returned to his seat he said, "It was a very bad idea." He seemed hurt but it passed quickly, and we all drank to the festival and to poetry.

Very late, back at the Metropol: We ran into Castro, Waldo, and Sergio and invited them up to our room, where I had a large bottle of white wine. The bar had closed. So we sat on our balcony and drank and laughed and talked and looked up at the starlit night sky.

There was something joyous yet lonely in our spirit. We needed to comfort each other. Later Fatty came up bringing signed copies of his own books. He stayed on after the others left and teased me about having been married more than once. In his country a man could marry as many women as he could afford but he could never divorce. He told us about his work as a newspaper writer. His poetry collections were read widely in schools in Egypt.

On this exciting night, Leopold Sedar Senghor had quietly arrived. From the balcony we could see the cars of his motorcade parked quietly in the darkness of the parking lot.

August 30! Morning before the big day! Save Cvetanovski (Yugoslav translator of Faulkner) presented me with translated copies of my two poems, "Blind Old Woman," and "Form," which I would read the following night at the Central Manifestation of the Festival, where Senghor would read and also receive the Golden Wreath. The Macedonian versions of the poems were simply for my own record. An actress had also received copies. I would read the poems in their original English.

After breakfast we went for the usual morning symposium. Predrag Matvejevic, a very popular figure at the festival, was speaking on Yugoslavia's literature of rebellion and resistance.

When Metvejevic finished, an Oriya Indian Poet, Sitakant Mahapatra, spoke on the problems and joys he had encountered while translating primitive Oriya poetry for the four anthologies of it he had published in his country. Mahapatra, author of three separate volumes of his own poetry, generally dismissed "self-indulgent" trends in European literature, strongly insisting on a functional art, giving the example of the tribal poetry of the Oriya as a fine example of useful art. I sat there listening and wondering. Surely it was a matter of definition. He mentioned Rimbaud, surprised at how a brilliant poet such as Rimbaud could be so self-indulgent. I finally decided that the art of Mahapatra's primitive communities was probably no more useful to the Oriya then Rimbaud was to the French, which is to say they each were extremely useful, though in different ways. Even the most self-indulgent art—if it's art—is useful.

Mahapatra and another Indian poet, K. Ayyappa Paniker, joined Sharyn and me for lunch at the Metropol. We talked out some of these ideas and I discovered we didn't really disagree as much as I thought we might. We talked about reality. Later, Paniker gave me a copy of the Indian magazine *Chitram,* in which he had published an article. In it he says, "I know what reality is. It is what I imagine to be real. And art at its most sublime is the creation of that reality." Repeat: *the creation of that reality. My* own ideas coming back at me. A nonrepresentational art. It was the position, years ago, that Senghor had also taken when defending the flexibility of African languages as a medium for poetry. It is the position the innovative fiction writers in America take: art is an extension of reality, not a mirror image of it. As such, it has spiritual, emotional, psychological, and utilitarian functions.

That night there was a concert in an ancient church, Saint Sophie, held in honor of Senghor. Senghor sat stiffly throughout the entire occasion. Then he and his entourage marched out under the glare of clicking cameras and bright lights. Following this we all went to a special dinner party, also in Senghor's honor, and sitting at our table were our usual friends, plus quite a few others. One was a top official of the festival who had not especially liked the idea of Senghor getting the Golden Wreath. Apparently the prize for Senghor had been pushed by the former ambassador to Senegal, who also happened to be Senghor's Macedonian translator.

There were more than 150 official guests from 25 countries, including Greece, France, Russia, and Hungary. There were hundreds of officials, members of the press, unofficial visitors, and friends of the festival. On the morning of August 31, only about a fourth of us were transported by yacht to the area of Saint Naum's Monastery on the shores of Lake Ohrid, where we all unloaded, ate, and drank lots of wine. We danced folk dances to the quaint music of little old men standing erect under weeping willows playing violins too loudly. Of our group I was first to join the Yugoslavs in their dance, then Nelljean took my hand, then Sharyn, then Kjell-Erik and Castro and Homero—everybody, I think, joined in, dancing around in a fantastic circle and singing and yelling.

Soon Senghor and his party joined us and the dancing stopped. The music became more formal. But a good feeling was still in the air despite so many uniformed guards and bodyguards standing at the edges of the area. Senghor, at one point, stood up from the table they had set for him under a willow. He said something kind about the occasion and the festival in general. Then, with his party and his beautiful French wife at his side, he started out. At this point, the president of the festival grabbed my hand and pushed it into Senghor's, and we, in this way, found ourselves shaking hands and smiling at each other. In French the president explained who I was and Senghor immediately spoke in English, saying he admired black American poets and was looking forward to hearing me read. Sharyn and Senghor then shook hands and exchanged greetings. We stepped back and others pushed toward him.

After Senghor left the picnic area, the fun started again. The dancing and the wine drinking and the music. Long tables with stacks of chicken, steaks, pork chops, salad greens, tomatoes, cheese, potato salad, fresh fruit lined the edges of the area. As soon as the tables ran low, members of the catering service would haul out more. Someone had a large book with clear pages. He was going about asking various guests to sign their names or write something in his book, perhaps a poem. Somebody gave me a pen and I closed my eyes, held my face toward the sky. People crowded around me, apparently watching my face, my closed eyes, then the page. Without looking I drew a picture of myself: It was expressionistic. Wow! They liked it. Were amazed. The owner of the book was delighted. Another person was circulating with a scrapbook of photographs he had taken of many of the official guests, asking them to sign their own pictures. A woman from Radio Skopje cornered me and reminded me that I had promised her a radio interview.

We found a quiet corner. To make a long story short, this is what I said in answer to her questions: The goal of literature is to operate as an extension of life. What did I think of literature that dealt with social revolution? I said it was all right if you could *show* me the message and not tell me *what* to think about it.

On the way back to Metropol I drifted into thoughts of Senghor. Senghor was one of the founders of the cultural theory called *negritude*. A man who'd spent time fighting for France, who'd spent time in a German prison camp. What had he said—"The object does not mean what it represents but what it suggests, what it creates." I closed my eyes, closing out the lake and the countryside and the mountains. A red sky shimmered before me. I felt Sharyn's hand softly curled into my own.

We were going back by bus. Waldo and Sergio sat across from us
and were telling Sharyn, in Spanish—they did not speak English—
about themselves, and Sharyn was translating everything said, and
when I said something to them, she'd translate it, and so on. Castro,
who spoke excellent English, was somewhere in the rear. He and
Homero had been two friends we had often depended on to help in
communicating with Sergio and Waldo. Waldo was a university professor in Santiago, Cuba. Sergio wanted to know the type of poetry I
wrote. Castro, on one occasion, took a very long time to explain to
Sergio my ideas and ideals in this area. Sergio smiled and said he wrote
mostly nature poetry. Now, they were good-naturedly laughing with
Sharyn about the "corny" music we had just heard at the picnic and
on the previous night at the Bristol. They reminded Sharyn of Latin
American friends she had hung out with at City College in New
York. Her enthusiasm was generated to me, and though I could not
speak well with them in their language nor in my own, I felt close to
them and cherished their friendship.

The Central Manifestation of the Struga Poetry Festival is called
"Bridges" because it takes place on a bridge. The whole city is brought
to a standstill. The entire occasion is televised. There were chairs for
special guests alongside the stage facing the river. Thousands, possibly
seven or eight thousand people, lined the river on both sides.
Television crewmen, newspaper photographers, ran around the outer
edges of the stage setting up equipment. Sharyn sat among the special
guests. Riet was there, too. Lassi Nummi's wife was also there.
Honorary members of the festival also held those seats. We, the poets,
were on the stage. Senghor arrived. A huge display of the Golden
Wreath decorated the back of the stage. Senghor was introduced and
praised for his contribution to literature, then presented the prize. He
came up on the stage from the right. He accepted the prize, said a few
words in French, then read a poem, an old poem written years ago. I
felt someone's elbow in my ribs. "He hasn't written a poem in thirty
years!" I tried to keep a straight face.

Fatty's reading was inspired and powerful; then I read, and there
was a tremendous ovation. I felt good. Really good. We all read: Waldo,
Homero, Hans, Kjell-Erik, Saadi, Nummi. After the affair, Senghor and
I talked briefly again while photographers snapped pictures. I gave him

an autographed copy of *The Dark and Feeling* and he was delighted, then signed a copy of his new Yugoslav collection for me. He felt that my reading and my poetry showed great sensitivity. I thanked him. Was happy that he liked the poems I had read.

Later that night, some friends from the American Embassy joined us at the Metropol for a late night snack. One felt that the poem "Form" which appears in *The Syncopated Cakewalk* was the most powerful attack on imperialism he had ever heard. When I explained that it was, in fact, quite literally a poem about language, about *form,* he blushed and said, "I guess I was just reading too much into it."

September 1. Breakfast with Frank and Eddy. Promises to meet again in Skopje at Hotel Grand.

We went downstairs. Homero was sitting in the lobby with his luggage at his knee. He gave us a sleepy smile. Most of our other friends were staying till the end. Tomorrow, the final day of the festival, September 2, some of them were scheduled to read at a theater in Skopje. But I had to get back: I had classes to teach. Homero, too, had to return to the Hague. Not realizing that the airport bus had already gone, we sat there waiting. The desk clerk did not offer any help or ask us any questions. A nervous taxi driver paced back and forth in the lobby. Only two others, a man and a woman, were waiting. What they were waiting for is anybody's guess. Finally, the taxi driver approached us. He wanted to take us to the airport. I waved him away, and went outside to look for the bus. No bus. He followed me saying, "Bus gone!" He said this over and over, waving his arms angrily. I kept waving him—and his words—away just as angrily.

Sharyn, Homero, and I finally gave in and took an overpriced taxi to the airport. On arrival, Homero was told he could not take the flight because he didn't have a ticket. He had only a reservation. It did not mean anything to them. Meanwhile, the morning flight to Belgrade had been delayed because of bad weather at Belgrade. This probably meant we would miss our flight to Frankfurt. As it turned out, we did. And because of the initial screw-up the remainder of the return trip was a nightmare not to be believed.

But once we were home, and I had slept nearly fifteen hours, in despair and exhaustion I lay there in bed knowing that the festival would stay with me as rare and good and important.

I AM READING MY POEMS

I am standing in the subway at Fourteenth Street and Sixth Avenue waiting for the D train uptown. Four trains go by. Still no D train. Something is wrong.

Then I see a sign that says—in small black print—that the D train comes on this track only between whateverhour to whateverhour, then same situation again later in the evening.

I am to be at Dodge High to read my poems at 8:50, and though I left home with time to get there (it is 8:50 now), I will be late. Frantic, I jump on the first train that comes—jump off at Thirty-fourth. Here I get on a D train, which has come from somewhere in one of those dark tunnels. On the way now. I begin to look over poems I may read. Make mental notes.

The school is big and impressive and on a street that goes down at an angle. I don't know the degree of that angle. A girl indicates the best door for quickest passage to room 324. Somebody named Mr. Herbert May's room.

Two ladies behind card tables on the first floor stop me, and tell me I need a pass to go upstairs. I have to go to the office for a pass.

The office is on the second floor. In the office, to get to May on third floor, I take the pass. I am starting up now. Then a fat, pleasant woman, who looks like a real poetry lover screams—"YOU MUST BE THE POET—MY GOD EVERYBODY'S WAITING FOR YOU—PLEASE COME WITH ME—I'LL SHOW YOU."

Meanwhile, two other ladies and a little smiling man in a dark blue suit stroll up and reach automatically for my hand. "Mr. Major, I'm Mr. May!" and we all go up in the elevator. Now we're going toward the room where about, let's see, probably 250 students are waiting quietly. It's a racially, religiously, culturally integrated school group.

They have a mike set up, boys with big impressive flash cameras, a tape recorder ready to go, and I give the pleasant fat woman, when she asks, the sheet of biographical data; she reads it in her shrill voice.

Meanwhile I'm taking off my coat, beginning to relax, but my throat is dry and they have no water in a glass ready for me, but I begin when she ends. I am reading a few short poems to warm up; I explain that most of these will be so short that each time I turn the page should indicate the end of each poem; and when I come to a poem that has a title I'll of course stop and carefully read it so you'll not think the title is just another line.

So I am going on now picking out short, quiet poems, mostly new things in the sense that they have been recently rewritten; I read one or two medium-size poems before stopping to say "My throat is dry," and a boy rushes out of the room and dashes back with a paper cup filled with water. "Thank you," I say, and continue. I get to a long poem, I stop, ask how much time we have; we now have five minutes left, and I get the long poem, entitled "Swallow the Lake" almost finished while the bell is ringing; the nice, fat woman cautions the students to remain seated and I am now finishing the last few lines, the end of the poem, now.

Everybody claps, stands up. The gentle black girl with intelligent eyes who is the editor of the school's literary mag comes up to me. "May I ask you a few questions?" Sure. "What d'you have planned for the future?" Immediate future? "Yes." Well. I plan to go to Mexico for a couple of months this summer for a long overdue vacation, before coming back to work in September.

Meanwhile Mr. May is showing me snapshots of myself that had been taken during the reading. They'll be in the school paper, we'll send you a copy. Okay? And someone else is touching my arm, saying "Let's go into the office and talk. You must be a very busy person." I walk with them. People thick all around me. But pleasant faces. Nice voices. They care about poetry. The reporter asks a few more questions about how and why I read, and I think I go into a brief thing about pacing and the verbal adjustment to the particular poem.

And Mr. May is now walking me two blocks down the street to the bus stop, talking about everything, even William Carlos Williams. He's very excited about poetry and wants me to come back, and who should he contact, me or the Academy? And I am saying, the Academy, and now the bus is coming and he's waving goodbye.

HALSEY JUNIOR HIGH 296—MAY 29, 1968

Mr. Jack Arenstein, the Assistant Principal, meets me in the hall. We're going up to the library where the students (perhaps forty or fifty) are waiting.

He's now introducing me and I am now speaking briefly about emotion in the human voice, the art of reading poetry, what I'm not going to do, and about what I am going to do; I talk about dramatic readings, actors, the quality of intellectual activity they as an audience have to engage in. They will have to lend their emotion to some of the poems because I am going to read in an even voice.

Meanwhile Mr. Arenstein is refereeing. I read one long poem, one of my best. He wants to know if they can stop me to have me analyze each poem. No, but later I'll talk about poetry, creativity in general. Won't try to critically evaluate any specific poem, here, now. The librarian, a black woman who constantly has this knowing smile at the corners of her mouth, is here. The school seems to be racially mixed, heavily Spanish, but a few of the black students ask questions like, "Have you written about things like racial problems?" I say some of my poems are concerned with racial problems. "Have you written about Martin Luther King?" Not a poem, but I wrote an article about him not long ago.

The questions pour out. Between them I read one, two, maybe three poems. The questions come again. "What do you mean by form, Mr. Major?" Arenstein pumps. I mean the physiological processes of the poem. I explain in detail.

I read several more poems. There are some questions about mood. I explain that I don't give much importance to mood, that students are carried away with the idea that one has to be in a certain mood to write a poem. I can work at poems six to eight hours a day, and not destroy the original mood of a poem.

"Can you make a living as a poet?" Yes, yes you can, but not from poetry itself. You can make a living being a poet. Later Arenstein says, "It's good for them to meet a writer who makes a living writing."

Some of the questions are sensible, many are simply obscure. I read two more poems that get to them. I can see from the recent questions they're worried about my strange rhythms, even my ideas about form. But not much.

Anyway, they're all very excited by the reading, the questions, my answers to the questions. The bell rings. Mr. Arenstein says: "WE'VE MILKED MR. MAJOR FOR SO MUCH VITAL INFORMATION AND HE'S BEEN SO GOOD TO COME HERE AND TAKE TIME OUT FROM HIS BUSY SCHEDULE TO READ HIS WORK TO US AND TO TALK TO US. LET'S GIVE HIM A BIG HAND," and they go to it.

Several students follow me downstairs, asking questions about how to become famous, how to get started being a poet.

JANE ADDAMS VOCATIONAL HIGH SCHOOL—JUNE 3, 1968

The head of the Department of English, Mrs. Margaret Reardon, comes down to the office where I'm waiting for her, but I step out a second for a drink of water and we miss each other for a minute. It's funny, so many doors.

But I'm very early, and finally she and I get together. "Here's the room, this is the music room," she says. "We'll hold the reading here. This is an all-girls school, a lot of the girls are studying beauty culture, home economics, things like that." She seems very decent, compassionate. She takes me around to the library to meet the librarian, also a nice woman. The bell finally sounds and we go around to the music room, and the girls are really jammed in there. She stands before them and she introduces me.

Meanwhile the principal, a man, comes in. "May I stay for a while?" Sure. "I had a beard like yours last summer while on my vacation." I smile. I begin to talk a little about my style—not just poetry style. Warm them up. Loosen them up. I read several poems and finally break the ice, get them smiling, asking questions freely, exchanging ideas. It is going well.

The principal leaves. The librarian also must return to her duties. We go on. The girls are really involved in the reading. They are truly listening to the poems. I tell them in some instances what inspired the poems. We even go a little overtime. It is raining outside. We are all happy. Two girls get excited enough to write poems of their own right on the spot. They later show them to me. And I leave happy to have been there.

PART TWO: VIEWS

TIGHTROPE-WALKING: A HUNDRED YEARS OF AFRICAN AMERICAN SHORT STORIES

V. F. Calverton, in the introduction to his landmark *Anthology of American Negro Literature* (New York: The Modern Libraray, Inc., 1929), said that the Negro "gave to whatever [cultural forms] he took [from the West] a new style and a new interpretation."

To showcase my conviction that Calverton was right, in 1992 I decided to edit an anthology of African American short stories. As a teacher I'd been unsatisfied with the then available choices. *Calling the Wind* (New York: HarperCollins, Inc., 1993) was the result. This essay served as its introduction. I wanted the collection to represent my deep convictions about the form.

Short stories, I discovered early in my teaching career, worked well as tools for learning. Over the years I tested many stories by black writers in the classroom. At a certain point, it seemed natural to collect in book form those most interesting, effective, and successful with students. One Chinese student, for example, discovered in a Richard Wright story a whole world that reminded him of the life of his grandparents in China. A young woman of Irish German descent, concerned about the rights of women, saw in Zora Neale Hurston's "The Gilded Six-Bits," Dorothy West's "Jack in the Pot," Toni Cade Bambara's "The Lesson," and Cyrus Colter's "The Lookout," the means to a strategy for discussing the relation between women, money, and power. A Mexican American, at the end of one of my courses, told me most of the stories, in one way or another, gave him insight into the behavior of members of his own family and community. Time and again I saw evidence of how these stories turned students on and, in some cases, even changed their lives.

Although the short story has roots in the oral traditions of any number of ancient civilizations, its beginnings as a formal literary genre in America are usually traced to Nathaniel Hawthorne, Washington Irving, and Edgar Allan Poe, who began consciously to develop and define the short story as a written form.

Poe laid out a blueprint: The short story was a "prose narrative" that necessarily had its own "magnitude": ordinarily, one should be able to read a short story in, say, half an hour. In any case, it shouldn't take a reader more than two hours to finish, for the idea was to create "a single effect." According to Poe, an "air of consequence or causation" must pervade the short story for it to work impressively. This was achieved through strict observance of certain principles of composition, as described in his essay "The Philosophy of Composition" and elsewhere:

> Nothing is more clear than that every plot, worth the name, must be elaborated to its dénouement before anything be attempted with the pen. It is only with the dénouement constantly in view that we can give a plot its indispensable air of consequence, or causation, by making the incidents, and especially the tone at all points, tend to the development of the intention.

Poe's prescription amounts to a kind of tightrope-walking for both the writer (in the process of construction) and the reader (in the process of reinventing the story as his or her own). The successful traditional short story aims for effect while creating its own universe, with emphasis on the complete unity—especially the tonal unity—of its parts. But by the 1920s the idea of the short story as an exemplary form with strict adherence to a single effect or single dramatic pattern, especially to the point of sacrificing plausibility, began to be challenged.

During that period the notion of an abstract, ideal model of the short story, insofar as it existed in Poe's and Hawthorne's days, began to lose ground as a working referent. The form opened up as readers and writers alike turned to the short story to fulfill all kinds of needs.

Some saw stories as paradigms of their own experience. Others appreciated the psychological or spiritual illumination found in them. Still others enjoyed the short story on a purely aesthetic level, as an artful play of language, a shimmer of verbal energy made visible. And many turned to the form to explore—some might say escape to—fascinating worlds vastly different from their own.

The modern American short story, then, came to be defined as any effective short prose piece built on a series of repeated verbal signs, images, and symbols, adding up to a subject matter—which, at its simplest level, refers to the most frequent activity in the story—while what we call *theme* emerges as a recurrent commentary, either straightforward or imagistic, on the quality or meaning of that activity. But every good short story presents its own magic, and it usually defies formula. It creates its own reality. This is not to say that stories have no bearing on the reader's (or writer's) reality; one of the first things I tend to say to a literature class is, "I think we can begin from the assumption that storytelling is vital to human health. It gives us workable metaphors for our lives." And one of my purposes in editing *Calling the Wind* was to to gather a group of stories that offers a wide range of workable metaphors for the ways we live.

My own discovery of African American writers happened during my last year of elementary school in Chicago. The discovery didn't take place in a classroom, and it occurred long after I had developed a love for reading and had been reading on my own—books I wanted to read, like J. D. Salinger's *The Catcher in the Rye* and *Nine Stories*—and not simply stories I had to read for classes.

I suspected there were writers whose cultural heritage was similar to my own, but we never had occasion to read any in class, even though most of my teachers were themselves of the same heritage. To most Americans, even college-educated Americans, African American literature was invisible. Even now, I still hear many of my students—most of them white—express surprise when they discover African American writers other than Richard Wright, James Baldwin, and Alice Walker.

This is despite the unmistakable influence of other black cultural forms—such as blues and jazz and popular black idioms—on American culture in general, and despite the fact that the African American literary anthology has had a relatively long publishing history. Those collections published in the 1920s, 1930s, and 1940s are now classic landmarks and historical keys to the cultural and artistic temperament of their moments in time. Although many of them are filled with works that Richard Wright, in his essay "Blueprint for Negro Writing," called "humble novels, poems and plays, prim and decorous ambassadors who went a-begging to white America," they nevertheless brought together the scattered and neglected—often privately published efforts—of Negro writers whose work might otherwise have been lost. They asserted and reasserted the presence of African American stories, poems, plays, and essays, keeping important names and works before an intensely interested, if relatively small, American reading audience.

I came across such anthologies around the same time I discovered Richard Wright's *Native Son* and Chester Himes's *The Third Generation*. A whole new world of cultural interpretation opened up. I soon was reading William Gardner Smith's *The Stone Face* and James Baldwin's *Go Tell It on the Mountain*. Inspired by the example of these works, I began trying to write my own stories.

African American writers have practiced the short story form with vigor, skill, and originality since the latter part of the nineteenth century. Like writers of European descent—writers such as Hemingway, Faulkner, Katherine Anne Porter, and Flannery O'Connor—writers of African descent found the form particularly suitable for capturing highly focused moments in the life of a vast and complex country. But average American readers, if they know anything at all about African American literature, usually hold a view of it fashioned by the politics of race and media stereotypes. It's a view based largely on myths and assumptions about African Americans handed down generation after generation, not only among Anglo-Americans but among almost all ethnic groups in this country. In her story "Recitatif," Toni Morrison deliberately sets out to deny readers any access to such racial stereotyping. As she points out in her wonderful little book *Playing in the Dark* (Cambridge, MA.: Harvard University Press, 1992), the story was "an experiment in the removal of all racial codes from a narrative about two characters of different races for whom racial identity is crucial." The writers gathered in this book collectively challenge the tendency Morrison set out to circumvent: the tendency to stereotype the Other.

Calling the Wind is the first trade anthology composed exclusively of twentieth-century African American short stories since Langston Hughes's *The Best Short Stories by Negro Writers: An Anthology from 1899 to the Present,* published in 1967. In making the selections, I wanted to include stories that met Poe's definition of the short story as well as stories that effectively *defied* not just his definition but other conventions. I wanted both to indicate the full diversity of African American work over the years and to show how the work of black writers has evolved, along with "mainstream" work, from earlier, formal practices of the genre to the present. But because of the complex history of this country, it is important to examine, at least briefly, some of the factors—elementary as they may be—that make up not just the literary, but the social and political context in which this particular selection exists.

First, what is an African American? For that matter, what is an American? And if this selection represents "ethnic" literature, what is "ethnic" literature? If asked to describe an American, most people around the world would almost reflexively describe a white person from North America. Whiteness in North America, however, is primarily a matter of not being black. In an essay titled "Our Greatest Gift to America," published in Calverton's 1929 anthology (pp. 410-12), journalist and novelist George S. Schuyler gives a stinging definition of white America and how it got that way:

> It is fairly well established, I think, that our [black] presence in the Great Republic has been of incalculable psychological value to the masses of white citizens. Descendants of convicts, serfs and half-wits, with the rest have been buoyed up and greatly exalted by being constantly assured of their superiority to all other races and their equality with each other. On the stages of a thousand music halls, they have had their vanity tickled by blackface performers parading the idiocies of mythical black roustabouts and rustics. Between belly-cracking guffaws they have secretly con-

gratulated themselves on the fact that they are not like these buffoons. Their books and magazines have told them, or insinuated, that morality, beauty, refinement and culture are restricted to Caucasians. On every hand they have seen smokes endeavoring to change from black to white, and from kinky hair to straight, by means of deleterious chemicals, and constantly they hear the Negroes urging each other to do this and that "like white folks." Nor do the crackers fail to observe, either, that pink epidermis is as highly treasured among blacks as in Nordic America, and that the most devastating charge that one Negro can make against another is that "he acts just like a nigger." Anything excellent they hear labeled by the race conscious Negroes as "like white folks," nor is it unusual for them, while loitering in the Negro ghetto, to hear black women compared to Fords, mulatto women to Cadillacs and white women to Packards. With so much flattery it is no wonder that the Caucasians have a very high opinion of themselves and attempt to live up to the lofty niche in which the Negroes have placed them. We should not marvel that every white elevator operator, school teacher and bricklayer identifies himself with Shakespeare, Julius Caesar, Napoleon, Newton, Edison, Wagner, Tennyson and Rembrandt as creators of this great civilization. As a result we have our American society, where everybody who sports a pink color believes himself to be the equal of all other whites by virtue of his lack of skin pigmentation, and his classic Caucasian features.

It is not surprising then, that democracy has worked better in this country than elsewhere. This belief in the equality of all white folks—making skin color the gauge of worth and the measure of citizenship rights—has caused the lowest to strive to become among the highest. Because of this great ferment, America has become the Utopia of the material world; the land of hope and opportunity. Without the transplanted African in their midst to bolster up the illusion, America would have

unquestionably been a very different place; but instead
the shine has served as a mudsill upon which all white
people alike can stand and reach toward the stars. I submit that here is the gift par excellence of the Negro in
America. To spur ten times our number on to great
heights of achievement; to spare the nation the enervat-
ing presence of a destructive social caste system, such as
exists elsewhere, by substituting a color caste system that
roused the hope and pride of teeming millions of ofays—
this indeed is a gift of which we can well be proud.

Despite the fact that Schuyler's tone is bitingly satiric and the words were
written sixty-three years ago, his thesis—"Without the transplanted
African in their midst to bolster up the illusion, America would have
unquestionably been a very different place"—agrees completely with
Toni Morrison's analysis. In *Playing in the Dark* (p. 65), Morrison says:

The presence of black people is inherent, along with gender and family ties, in the earliest lesson every child is
taught regarding his or her distinctiveness. Africanism is
inextricable from the definition of Americanness—from
its origins on through its integrated or disintegrating
twentieth-century self.

In other words, the very presence of an Other (in this case a dark, contrasting Other) helps to shape the popular (white) definition of an
American self. This dark other presence, again in Morrison's words
(p. 17), has a profoundly complex function:

Through the simple expedient of demonizing and reify-
ing the range of color on a palette, American Africanism
makes it possible to say and not say, to inscribe and erase,
to escape and engage, to act out and act on, to historicize
and render timeless. It provides a way of contemplating
chaos and civilization, desire and fear, and a mechanism
for testing the problems and blessings of freedom.

This white image, contrasted against the black Other, is in fact only a mythic American. The American presence is so varied and so complex that exchange and conflict between the black image and the white image tend absurdly to diminish the richness of a network of ethnic cultures that truly is the American human landscape. Most individuals in these groups feel some sense of doubleness, feel their otherness and their Americanness. One indication of an internal struggle can be seen in their tendency to hyphenate the names signaling the two different selves—African-American, Native-American, Asian-American, Mexican-American, and so on.

W. E. B. Du Bois, in *The Souls of Black Folk* (1903), wrote (p. 45):

> It is a peculiar sensation, this double-consciousness, this sense of always looking at one's self through the eyes of others, of measuring one's soul by the tape of a world that looks on in amused contempt and pity. One ever feels his twoness—an American, a Negro; two souls, two thoughts, two unreconciled strivings; two warring ideals in one dark body; whose dogged strength alone keeps it from being torn asunder.

Since Americans all, originally, came from somewhere else, this doubleness, as Jack Hicks points out in *In the Singer's Temple* (1981; p. 84),

> lies at the heart of the American experience. At best an uneasy and shifting peace. To stress one's national and ethnic origins and culture or to conceive oneself as purely an American, cut from the ties of people and past—these are truly warring ideals, the poles of total assimilation and the supreme isolation of place, race, and class that have generated the tension defining our national struggles.

So to some degree doubleness describes the condition of all Americans, whether or not they know it.

Some researchers argue that since Anglo-Americans and descendants of Western Europe constitute this new, invented "white American" that Toni Morrison talks about, they set the agenda for the culture of the country. However, no human activity is ever that simple. The idea of being American is still new to even "white" Americans.

Among the many theories about the origins of Anglo-American feelings of selfhood is one that centers on social and cultural transformations made by the Puritans of New England. But the Puritans present only one example of many such transformations, in the colonies and afterward. Very likely a national sense of identity did not take hold on a massive scale until after World War I. Apparently, at that point, a sense of self among Americans was enforced—from the outside—by the enormous pressure of this worldwide action, which served at least to show Americans what they had in common and how they were different from peoples of other countries.

Television, it seems to me, became the other source of solidifying an American sense of selfhood. But that is another story. The African American journey to selfhood was always deeply ironic. Africans and people of African descent were subjected to legal and illegal slavery in the "land of liberty." And this "new world" was already an old world long inhabited by peoples—commonly called Indians—the Africans immediately identified with, especially in the Deep South. It's little wonder that such a historical experience would produce an ethnic population whose writers seemed instinctively to write stories with irony at their core.

If we can call any literature ethnic—that is, if it can be defined in cultural terms—then we can say it's the element of regionalism in the work that opens it to such a definition. I use the word "regionalism" with its connotations of the homespun, the local, the rural, the provincial, the narrow; even the unrefined. Werner Sollers, in *Beyond Ethnicity* (1986), uses the word "parochialism" to imply the same sort of limitations. Sollers says, "Ethnic writing is equated with parochialism and ethnic writers who are not parochial are classified not as ethnic but as 'wholly' American." He goes on to say that

> a broader and more inclusive definition of ethnic literature is helpful: works written by, about, or for persons who perceive themselves, or were perceived by others, as members of ethnic groups, including even nationally and internationally popular writings by "major" authors and formally intricate and modernist texts.

William Boelhower, in *Through a Glass Darkly* (1984), argues that all American literature is ethnic. In other words, Boelhower seems to suggest that no American personality is so generic that it has lost ethnic memory of a previous cultural life in Europe or Africa or China or India or South America or somewhere else.

When we say Americans live in a multi-ethnic or poly-ethnic society, we are acknowledging the truth of Hicks's comments on doubleness. The writers represented here grew up with a strong sense of it. Cultural doubleness is common among ethnic groups throughout the world. America, Russia, Yugoslavia, Italy, and other relatively recent federations are filled with peoples with divided cultural—to say nothing of political—allegiances. Cultural homogenization, such as it exists anywhere, is usually the by-product of power seeking and plunder.

Just as irony is a key to the African American experience, so it is an important device in African American literature. While all good fiction is, on one level or another, ironic, many of the stories here pointedly deal with situations that appear to be one thing but are revealed in the end to be another—as in James Alan McPherson's "The Story of a Scar" (1973). In other instances the subtext of a story may all along be something quite different from what the story appears to say on the surface—as in Chesnutt's "The Goophered Grapevine" (1899) and Ralph Ellison's "Flying Home" (1944). These stories might also be read as allegories or parodies or satire, but in each case they partake of situational irony. That is, the ironic incident makes a moral judgment about—and effectively manipulates—the temporal or social context of the model incident, even as the ironic incident is measured against its model or ideal. In other words, an ironic situation usually comes into focus when juxtaposed with what we believe to be a stable, recognizable, predictable—and therefore usually preferred—reality.

Chesnutt's, Ellison's, and McPherson's stories share another device: Each incorporates a story told within the story. All three are therefore, among other things, about storytelling.

"The Goophered Grapevine," a parody of the plantation story, is about talking and listening, and its theme is deception—deceptive talking, deceptive listening. The outer, framing story is in the apparently authoritative but ultimately unreliable narrative voice of a young

liberal white man from the North named John. The inner story, told
by Uncle Julius—which, on the surface, seems to lack credibility—by
contrast gains an ironic authority even as the old ex-slave insists that
the visitors from up North really are not required to believe what he's
about to tell them. Uncle Julius's aim is to make the visitor feel comfortable with their assumed prejudices, and he clearly reinforces any
possible stereotypes they might hold about his people by going on to
say that all Negroes love possum, chicken, and watermelon. Paul
Laurence Dunbar called this act "wearing the mask."

Uncle Julius talks first about the former plantation owner's struggle to keep the slaves from eating the scuppernong grapes he grows
to make wine; in order to accomplish his goal the owner, Mr.
McAdoo, finally resorts to hiring a conjure woman called Aunt
Peggy. The second part of Julius's story involves McAdoo's purchase
of an elderly slave named Henry, who defies the goopher and eats the
summer grapes but does not suffer the expected consequences. Using
one of Aunt Peggy's potions made from the sap of the grapevine,
Henry is instead transformed into a strong young man. Leave it to
McAdoo to find in this a fine business opportunity: He sells Henry
at a high price. Winter comes, Henry turns into an old man again,
and thereupon McAdoo buys him back cheap. The slaveholder keeps
this up for a number of years. Each spring Henry becomes young
again; McAdoo sells him while he's strong and vigorous and then
buys him back in the winter when he's old and bent. In this way the
slaveholder increases his wealth.

Of course Uncle Julius's story is an entertaining attempt to dis-
suade John from buying the McAdoo plantation with its conjured
fields: neglected since the Civil War ended a few years before, the
plantation is Julius's home, pathetic as it may be. But the shrewd old
man's story of the plantation's heyday is also a celebration of the
African American tall tale and a satire of the nostalgic and sentimental stories about slave and slaveholder relations so popular during
Reconstruction. And while Uncle Julius does not leave any noticeable
impression on John, John's wife, Annie, recognizes Uncle Julius's
humanity and courage and is renewed by them.

In Ellison's "Flying Home," set in the 1940s, a young black man
named Todd crashes his fighter plane in a white man's field. He's dis-

covered by an old black man and a boy. The story lends itself to many different critical approaches and has literary roots in a number of ancient stories—the death and rebirth of the phoenix, in the Icarus and Daedalus story of ill-fated flight, and in the biblical stories of the Fall as well as the Prodigal Son. In its ironic structure, "Flying Home" bears a resemblance to Chesnutt's story of forty-five years before.

Jefferson, the narrator of the inner story, seems at the opening to be a simpleminded, childlike old man, much like Uncle Julius. Nevertheless it is his folksy wisdom that becomes the means by which Todd, the protagonist, rediscovers his abandoned cultural self. Jefferson begins with the story of the buzzard. In African American folklore, the buzzard is a wily, popular totem, a bird that manages to survive on dead things, things others do not want, and he is often unjustly reviled for it. The buzzard story sheds light on Todd's story in a number of ways. As a fighter pilot Todd is a symbol of death; he has also been given second-class treatment by the military establishment he's attempted to serve. And in Jefferson's opinion, he is a creature who has ranged too far from home and from the security of his own cultural identity.

It is old Jefferson who turns out to be the educated young man's teacher and deliverer; through him Todd is finally lifted from his fall, literally and spiritually, and delivered back to the bosom of his culture. As a phoenix he is brought up out of sleep, out of a dream of a "bird of flaming gold," and the end of the story suggests that in this transformation Todd's sense of himself will undergo a dramatic positive change.

Like "Flying Home," McPherson's "The Story of a Scar" is also about a conversation between two black people of different classes—the narrator, who considers himself to be a man of taste, and a woman with a scarred face. When they meet in a doctor's waiting room and he asks her about the scar, the two launch themselves into a "capping" exchange. He sees her as a foolish woman who's wasted her time on a no-good roughneck of a man, a view that is psychologically oppressive and insulting. In Zora Neale Hurston's words, he sees her as "the mule of the world."

She is, however, well aware of the narrator's condescension, and she challenges him every step of the way in order to get her own story told. She has been involved with two men who work with her at the post office: one, Billy, is supposed to be a good, responsible adult; the

other, Teddy, an apparent no-account. So firm are the narrator's negative assumptions about the scarred woman and how she has come to
be so wounded that at first we assume he's reading her correctly. We
also assume that she is misjudging the narrator when she tells him
how intolerant, narrow-minded, and stubbornly set in his ways he is.

By the end we have changed our minds about both of them. We see
she is on target; he has completely—and viciously—misjudged her. In
the reader's eyes, she vindicates herself by forcing the narrator to confront
his prejudiced view of her. But the narrator's pretensions turn out to be
so uncomfortably close to those of the woman's attacker that we doubt
he will ultimately be changed by what the story of the scar has to teach.

Although irony is a strong element in these stories, others uti-
lize even bolder ironic strokes. In "The Ingrate" (1900), for example, Paul Laurence Dunbar demonstrates how a slaveholder's generosity in teaching his slave to write is simply another form of
exploitation in a threadbare disguise. We quickly see a wide gap
between the apparent reality of the situation and what the slaveholder professes to be the case. Even so, when the slave uses his new
skills to escape bondage, the slaveholder feels betrayed. Similarly, in
John Edgar Wideman's "Damballah" (1981), another slaveholder
convinces himself that he has been wronged when the protagonist
refuses to submit to a life of slavery. In both cases, self-deception
leads to self-righteous indignation.

Most of the stories here can be read and appreciated for their
varied and rich manipulations of verbal and structural irony, but they
can also, of course, be appreciated from any number of angles. Some
groupings suggest themselves immediately: Zora Neale Hurston's
"The Gilded Six-Bits" (1933), Dorothy West's "Jack in the Pot"
(1940), Cyrus Colter's "The Lookout" (1970), and Toni Cade
Bambara's "The Lesson" (1972) are all wise stories about the power
of money. Jean Toomer's "Esther" (1923) and Chester Himes's "The
Headwaiter" (1938) are stories about the individual in conflict with
himself or herself, or with his or her surroundings. Jessie Fauset's
"Mary Elizabeth" (1919), Langston Hughes's "Who's Passing for
Who?" (1952), William Melvin Kelley's "The Only Man on Liberty
Street" (1956), and John A. Williams's "Son in the Afternoon" (1962)
play on the complex psychology of gender, race, and class

differences. Each of these stories records some particulars of the black experience. Each also bears witness to the social and political sensibility of its time.

The African American short story is a product of a specific culture, but not one that developed in isolation. This more or less self-contained black culture would have evolved in America with or without legal segregation to coerce it. Its evolution was an act of survival. Built on sacred and secular foundations, black culture interacted with the larger mainstream along lines acceptable primarily to the mainstream. This history of separateness—or, to put it more harshly, alienation and segregation—alone justifies the act of gathering the writings of writers who, whether loosely or narrowly, can be called African American.

These writers, then, are men and women whose visions were shaped by growing up somewhere in the United States or, if they were born elsewhere, by living as black people in this country. Their differences are as important as what they share. In an essay titled "Remembering Richard Wright" (*Going to the Territory*, 1986), Ralph Ellison makes an important point about the role of geography in the shaping of "fate." Ellison points out that because he grew up in the Southwest, he and Wright—who grew up in the Southeast—were "divided by geography and a difference of experience based thereupon."

If the social experiences of black Americans vary from region to region, the historical stages vary as much, and it's important to remember the aesthetic and social philosophies, the *complexity*, of each period of African American literature. These have been defined as Antebellum (1853-1865), Postbellum (1865-1902), the period of the Old Guard (1902-1917), the Harlem Renaissance (1917-1929), and the period of Social Protest (1929-1959).

While each period had its overriding concerns, two social and political tendencies were more or less always present in African American thought, and both were addressed to the problem of racial oppression. One was the quest for justice through racial integration with Anglo-Americans. The other was the quest for justice through geographical and/or psychological separation from Anglo-Americans. Both tendencies found expression in slave narratives and in essays, novels, poems, and short stories.

African American artists in many media have given explicit or subtle expression to these concerns, usually maintaining a high level of artistic excellence and avoiding the mere business of chronicling offenses.
Those concerns are vividly displayed in the short stories of the various
periods represented here. Writers of the Antebellum period, such as
William Wells Brown and Martin R. Delany, were primarily concerned
with informing a white audience of the injustices of slavery and racial
oppression. These writers were absolutely sure they understood the
meaning of freedom, understood it in the same way enslaved folk had
understood its importance since the beginning of civilization. They
hoped to find a humane way to tell white readers, preferably sympathetic white readers, about the crime of human bondage. A certain paradox
lay in this, and many of the early works were prefaced with apologetic
notes to the reader—shallow attempts to sugarcoat the just complaint.

The Postbellum period—which corresponds roughly with
Reconstruction (1865-1877) and its promise of social and cultural
prosperity—produced writers such as Paul Laurence Dunbar, Charles
Chesnutt, Sutton Griggs, W. E. B. Du Bois, and others. These writers
continued the attempt to educate a Eurocentric reading audience
about the racial nightmare in which those of African descent lived.
But they also began to write with the assumption that black consciousness and black culture were significant, self-evident entities in
the world, deserving of respect.

The African American short story formally begins with Dunbar
and Chesnutt. Chesnutt's "The Goophered Grapevine" and Dunbar's
"The Ingrate" speak directly to the social, psychological, and legal problems of black people before the turn of the century. W. E. B. Du Bois
and others spill over into the next period, that of the Old Guard. By
1917 the Old Guard represented rather conservative ideas and ideals
about African American culture in general. The contrast between their
positions and those of the next generation—the Harlem Renaissance—
is as sharp as a blade of light pouring down through a stained glass window. The aesthetic and political stance of Rudolph Fisher, Zora Neale
Hurston, Jean Toomer, Claude McKay, Nella Larsen, Wallace Thurman,
and Langston Hughes is well described by Hughes in his famous essay,
"The Negro Artist and the Racial Mountain," published in *The Nation*
(June 23, 1926). In part, Hughes says (p. 694):

> An artist must be free to choose what he does, certainly,
> but he must also never be afraid to do what he might
> choose. . . . We younger Negro artists who create now
> intend to express our individual dark-skinned selves with-
> out fear of shame. If white people are pleased we are glad.
> If they are not, it doesn't matter. We know we are beauti-
> ful. And ugly too. The tom-tom cries and the tom-tom
> laughs. If colored people are pleased we are glad. If they
> are not, their displeasure doesn't matter either. We build
> our temples for tomorrow, strong as we know how, and we
> stand on top of the mountain, free within ourselves.

That statement and the whole essay was, in effect, a manifesto and a declaration of independence. It was also a strike against what Hughes called the "smug Negro middle class."

The period I call Social Protest includes the Depression years of the 1930s and reaches into the 1940s and 1950s. Richard Wright was and is the best known black writer of this time. It was characterized by the rise of a healthy intellectual curiosity on the social and cultural Left. To many black writers, Marxism or some form of socialism looked, at least for a while, like a viable solution to the economic problems black people and the rest of the nation faced. More important, the advent of a truly classless society would inevitably mean an end to racism.

But political rifts in the nation as a whole widened through the 1960s, and by the end of the decade Black (Cultural) Nationalism began to replace the integrative impulse of the earlier era of protest. Separation from Anglo-American culture was not simply the only route to justice, it was itself the goal. While the political agenda of many of the poets and playwrights of the nationalist period caused them to create what now looks like the work of ideologues, few black fiction writers completely fell into step.

Du Bois said that all art is propaganda, but propaganda is not nec-essarily art. When the Black Nationalist theory of culture was applied to fiction, it was done in the narrowest possible—to use a currently popular word—Afrocentric terms, and it tended to be an uncomfort-able fit. The spirit of Black Nationalism, with its reactionary and conservative tendencies, was challenged by the diversity of such writers as Samuel R. Delany, Alice Walker, Henry Van Dyke, Ernest J. Gaines, James Alan McPherson, Paule Marshall, Charles Wright, John Edgar Wideman, and Al Young. These and other writers were creating an eclectic body of work that many critics took as a sign of a second "New Negro" Renaissance.

Again, in retrospect, it's possible to see that before the 1960s, African American writers of fiction more often than not chose race as their theme and racial conflict as their subject matter. They were primarily interested in the effects of white racism on the lives of black people, but by the mid-1970s that was no longer the case. In the past two decades, black American artists have continued to be concerned with racial conflict, with racism, and with the rich ironies of American history and culture in what is oversimplified as the Black Experience, but they probe beyond its merely political aspects to find the roots that link their experience to all human experience. These novelists and poets and playwrights and short story writers have probed the "human universals" through the cultural particulars. Ralph Ellison, in the 1982 introduction (p. XX) to the thirtieth anniversary edition of *Invisible Man* (1952), brings this impulse into focus in one neat sentence:

> [My] task was one of revealing the human universals hid-
> den within the plight of one who was born black and
> American, and not only as a means of conveying my per-
> sonal vision of possibility, but as a way of dealing with the
> sheer rhetorical challenge involved in communicating
> across our barriers of race and religion, class, color and
> region—barriers which consist of the many strategies of
> division that were designed, and still function, to prevent
> what would otherwise have been a more or less natural
> recognition of the reality of black and white fraternity.

Tied into the web of assumptions and half-truths that make up an American's sense of reality is a denial of the history of actual black and white relations, intimate and otherwise, in this land. The possible "fraternity" Ellison speaks of is further eclipsed by this historical denial of the importance of black people in the shaping of white American reality and identity. Toni Morrison, again, makes the point well (*Playing in the Dark,* p. 44):

> I want to suggest that . . . autonomy, authority, newness and difference, absolute power . . . not only became the major themes and presumptions of American literature, but that each one is made possible by, shaped by, activated by a complex awareness and employment of a constituted Africanism. It was this Africanism, deployed as rawness and savagery, that provided the staging ground and arena for the elaboration of the quintessential American identity.

Part of the American reality is, as James Baldwin often pointed out, that black people and white people in America are kissing cousins. Many of these short stories stand as testimony to that truth, to that troubled bond—troubled because the first time an enslaver forced himself upon his slave, though he failed to recognize it (or his own barbarism), he was acknowledging the slave's humanity, that which he officially denied. From that moment on, the failure of slavery was assured.

And, irony on irony, the denial of kinship is so sternly expressed both in public life and in mainstream literature that the denial warps the American psyche. This exchange and conflict has been a great double-edged challenge facing the serious American writer for nearly two centuries, and it remains so to this day.

RHYTHM: A HUNDRED YEARS
OF AFRICAN AMERICAN POETRY

Why poetry? And, anyway what is poetry? We need poetry because it speaks to us in terms and rhythms most instinctive to our existence. Poetry has its basis in the very beating of our hearts, in the rhythm of our footfalls as we walk, and in the pattern of our breathing. It is the refinement made of our voices speaking in everyday terms.

Because of the importance of these rhythmic patterns, poetry is always as much about itself as it is about, say, the West Coast, van Gogh, violence, snapshots, paintings, fishing in a creek, riding a bike across a tightrope, being born, prison, slavery, menses, language, jazz, insomnia, self, death, or anything else you can think of.

One of the central things to poetry is metaphor, and there are a variety of metaphors—juxtaposed, past tense, positive, negative, double, triple, multiple, organic, non-organic, you name it. But its central functions are fairly consistent in all of its mutations: metaphor is about *equivalences,* especially of objects or ideas not commonly seen together or thought of as having similarities. Another way of saying this is to say that metaphor seeks to unearth an *assumed sameness* submerged in dissimilar objects or ideas. The implied analogy that metaphor makes between, say, a car and a lemon, is well-known. This is the basic business of metaphor.

Of equal importance is voice. In poetry voice can be everything. A poet without a good ear, without a sense of the music in speech, is like a snowstorm without snow. June Jordan grew up listening to the "Black English" of Harlem and Bedford Stuyvesant, Brooklyn, its syntax and grammar, its music, and listening to the "impeccable" jive talk of a favorite uncle who lived upstairs. Rita Dove, as a kid, listened to relatives and neighbors talking on the front porch, to the "women in the kitchen," listened to the pitch of voices at, say, a Fourth of July cookout, hearing the cadence of the speech, doing research without even knowing she was working. Yusef Komunyakaa chose poetry because of the "conciseness, the precision, the imagery, and the music in the lines." Cornelius Eady says he has an eye and an ear for the "music inside" the poem. He follows the direction that music takes. In a sense, he sees language everywhere: when people are talking he watches the way their hands move, and the way the light falls, and so on.

But to get back to metaphor. As one of the tropes, metaphor—especially complex metaphor—is a device in which the original object has at least two distinct functions. It not only changes our perception of the *compared object* but also continues to both change and represent *itself.* And metaphor, perhaps more than any other device of poetry, is on the best terms with the natural world while also being on equally good terms with the materials (language) out of which poetry is sculpted. In short, poetry is necessary.

Again—what do you *do* with poetry? And, anyway, *how* do you do what you do with poetry? The question isn't so much what is going on in the poem as it is what is going on between you and the poem. You *experience* poetry. If a poem can be taken as a "sonic entity," as Denise Levertov says, then we can read it the way we listen to music. Rita Dove has said:

> Poetry connects you to yourself, to the self that doesn't
> know how to talk or negotiate. We have emotions that
> we can't really talk about, and they're very strong. . . .
> I really don't think of poetry as being an intellectual
> activity. I think of it as a very visceral activity.

And this "visceral activity" we call poetry happens in time, the way music is experienced. Ernest Fenollosa said that poetic form is *regular* (like the heartbeat) and that its basic "reality" has to do with its existence in time.

And in the case of poetry on the page, we can say too that poetry, like painting, to some degree exists in space. It's both temporal and spatial.

Fenollosa says: "All arts follow the same law; refined harmony lies in the delicate balance of overtones." Powerful poetry that moves us has to be constructed with language that is in motion and vividly alive. It can fly and "quiver," as D. H. Lawrence felt it should. It can use the "real world" as Hart Crane believed. It can be closed or open in form. It can use breathing as a measuring device, as Charles Olson said. The poet can concentrate on the relationship between the mind and the ear, or give more attention to how the poem on the page strikes the eye.

Poetry is a "formal invention" (to use William Carlos Williams's phrase), and as such it is concerned with its own scheme, its design, the physical and tonal shape of language. And when it is most successful, it is composed of *things*—things held together or suspended together with tension and *in*tension. Abstractions such as ideas, concepts, emotions, or feelings, are also best rendered through the thingness of metaphor. Or as Pound put it in one of his three principles for writing poetry: "Direct treatment of the 'thing' whether subjective or objective." Or Williams: "No ideas but in things . . ." *(Paterson)*. Or Williams in an even more precise manner when he said: "A poem is a small (or large) machine made of words . . ." and because of the machinelike *thingness* of poetry "its movement is intrinsic . . . [and has] a physical more than a literary character."

Poetry, like myth and slang, may also be closer to our instinctive natures than we normally think of it being. It can, for example, be enacted in religious terms. Robert Hayden and Derek Walcott come to mind.

Robert Hayden believed poetry, though rendered in concrete terms, has a spiritual basis, that it is the poet's way of responding to the basic abstract questions—birth, death, love, the meaning of life, God, etc.—that concern "all human beings."

Hayden's interest in the essential mysteries shows throughout his work. Although, for him, Nature itself supplied many answers to the less difficult spiritual questions of life, Hayden seems to have reached a certain level of peace in the absence of absolute answers. He came to believe that suffering was essential to salvation, to deliverance, to sanctification.

Walcott, in a similar way, sees the *act* of writing poetry as a form of praying. In an interview, he said:

> I have never separated the writing of poetry from prayer. I have grown up believing it is a vocation, a religious vocation. . . . I imagine that all artists and all writers in that moment before they begin their working day . . . [find that] there is something about it votive and humble and in a sense ritual-istic . . . I mean, it's like the habit of Catholics going into water: you cross yourself before you go in. Any serious attempt to try to do something worthwhile is ritualistic.

Poetry discovered *me* when I was four or five. My mother wrote a poem for me and I had to recite it in church. Soon I was writing my own poems. This was during a time when my primary artistic expression was drawing, usually with crayons. We also called it "coloring." Since my command of the crayon was greater than my command of writing, in a sense, my drawings became my poems. Then at about the age of twelve—while still drawing and now painting with a passion—I seriously (too seriously!) committed myself to writing poetry. The idea was to be a full, rounded Renaissance artist: I would write, paint, compose music, invent things. I had my heroes and da Vinci was among them. Whatever authority I have in this area has its roots in those long-ago naive events.

In 1966, when I was twenty-nine, I published a statement called "Black Criterion," an early articulation of what later became known as the Black Aesthetics Movement. If I was among the first to make such a statement, I was also among the first to turn my back on the straightjacket philosophy of the movement because it represented an ideological prison for the artist. I could not see art's main function as a cultural arm of a political movement—which is what Black Nationalism taught. After all, it was already clear to me that art produced under political direction was pretty bad art. This is not the same thing as saying that I do not believe poetry can be, in the French sense, a means of *engagement*. It certainly can. An example of first-rate political poetry is Robert Hayden's "Middle Passage." It begins:

Sails flashing to the wind like weapons,
sharks following the moans the fever and the dying;
horror the corposant and compass rose.
Middle Passage:
    voyage through death
    to life upon these shores.

In a sense, then, I resolved the confusion in my heart and mind.
And in the words of Langston Hughes's famous 1926 essay manifesto,
"The Negro Artist and the Racial Mountain": "An artist must be free
to choose what he does . . . but he must also never be afraid to do what
he might choose." If black people were pleased, Hughes said, fine, if
white people were pleased, fine. If they weren't, to hell with them. The
way to the universal was through the particular. An old truth.

I found the spirit of Hughes's artistic rebelliousness much more
attractive than the military goose-stepping propaganda of sixties Black
Nationalism. I came to believe that poets (and writers) should feel free
to tap into a deeper truth than the important though not *all-important*
social or political aspects of experience.

I wanted to write *and to read* poetry that spoke from the depths
of what was most human, from the depths of what we *all* shared, not
merely from the levels where our differences could be detected. I
wanted political poetry that was organic in its ideas, a political poetry
that in no way compromised its own artistic nature.

But can poetry be both political or didactic and at the same time
still be art? Among recent African American poets, Audre Lorde, I
think, proved that it can. Sonia Sanchez, with her haiku-like style, in
her exploration of self in exchange and conflict with community, in
her probing of the personal self's relation to the public self, in her
search for the higher public good in that public self, in her constant
redefining of those selves, especially as female body and spirit, proves
that it is possible. Haki R. Madhubuti, too, in his militancy, in his black
pride, in his interest in family and culture, in his sociopolitical philosophy of the black community as a self-directed entity, in his interest
in the heroic black perspective, I think, proves that it can be done.
Jayne Cortez, with her improvisational free form, in her struggle to
define the black female in the context of family, class, body, spirit, and

moral self, proves that it's possible to focus on these social issues—as well as drug addiction, persecution, rape, war, sexism, racism—and create poems that stand on their own as works of solid art.

In other words, certainly by 1970, I firmly believed that political or social issues were legitimate subject matter. I saw my way clearly from there. I suspect my background as a painter compelled me to *see* language, almost as a plastic form, see it in a *direct* way—the way a painter confronts color and lines before visual narrative can become an issue—as the raw material of poetry-making, and to find a sense of urgency at this level rather than, say, in message.

Just now, in looking again at that little "essay," I noticed a key element—something I still believe, something that obviously came from a deeper place in me than most of what that essay represents—at its core:

> A work of art, a poem, can be a complete "thing"; it can be
> alone, not preaching, not trying to change men, and though
> it might change them, if the men are ready for it, the poem
> is not reduced in its artistic status. I mean we black poets
> can write poems of pure creative black energy right here in
> the white west and make them works of art without falling
> into the cheap marketplace of bullshit and propaganda.
> But it is a thin line to stand on.

In 1968—a politically and socially turbulent year—I edited an anthology called *The New Black Poetry* (1969) and wrote a strident introduction, one that, in retrospect, seems perfectly in tune with the hue and cry of that year—a year of infamous assassinations and insurrections on a grand scale. Composed of the works of seventy-six poets, the anthology somehow escaped the most obvious pitfall it faced: all of the poems might have been didactic but, perhaps for the same reason that the essential portion of my little essay escapes being pure propaganda, they are not.

And, in fact, only about ten percent of the poems fall into that category. I was pleased to notice that even the didactic or propagandistic poems in my anthology are good—not bad—political poems. Many of them are organic *and* engaged at the same time.

A good number of the poets included went on to become "high-profile," highly accomplished poets, such as Audre Lorde, June Jordan (then called June Meyer), Al Young, Ishmael Reed, Nikki Giovanni, Sonia Sanchez, and Ethridge Knight. (LeRoi Jones [Amiri Baraka] was already famous.) But editing the anthology taught me a lot—about poetry, about the politics of poetry.

The teaching (and learning) of poetry has long interested me. I taught my first formal poetry course at City University of New York-Brooklyn College in 1968, when I was thirty-one, under the umbrella of something called the SEEK program. Adrienne Rich was teaching in the same program. We were not *real* college professors—at that time at least—and had been brought in strictly as poets. The anthology I hastily selected and used (hopefully, less hastily) was my first mistake. I've forgotten the title and the editor, although I do remember that she was not a poet but a junior high school teacher in the Bronx. It could not have been worse. Uneven in quality, I came to hate it, and all but abandoned it two-thirds of the way through the course. This threw me back on my own resources, and in the final third of the course there was some noticeable improvement.

But I did learn a couple of things from that initial experience. A good anthology is essential, and the poem, like the short story, is a powerful and useful thing to place before students. They can, as William Carlos Williams indicated, perish from lack of what they will find there. My objective, then, was for this anthology *The Garden Thrives* (my second poetry anthology) to serve the general reader and to be a good teaching tool for the enjoyment and examination of this country's twentieth-century African American poetry, which is an essential aspect of American Literature.

African American literature, formally speaking, is perhaps best known for its vast body of diverse and often brilliant poetry. This has a lot to do with poetry's relationship to music—another cultural form in which black Americans, from the beginning of their presence in this country, have worked joyously. (Autobiographies—including slave narratives—run a close second.)

It's ironic that there were black poets born slaves—Lucy Terry, Jupiter Hammon, Phillis Wheatley—who were writing and publishing their poetry on these shores or in England in the eighteenth century, a time when slave ships were still unloading their captured or purchased cargo to be sold as property. Ironic because the European explanation for slavery was rooted in the Christian belief that Africans were subhuman, incapable of learning anything requiring abstract thinking. The legacies of this belief and that institution linger stormily in the hearts of Americans even now.

Today, in the sophisticated and complex poetry of Rita Dove, Michael Harper, Derek Walcott, Ai, Jay Wright, or Audre Lorde, thematically speaking, tribal or folk elements and the universals are obvious. In fact, such elements are ironically more in evidence in the twentieth century, and especially since the mid-1940s, than in the efforts of Lucy Terry, Jupiter Hammon, or Phillis Wheatley.

Lucy Terry was the first known African slave on these shores to write a poem in English, "Bars Fight," (1746), about an Indian "ambush" in Deerfield, Massachusetts that same year. The poem describes, among other things, Samuel Allen's resistance and his death. (The bars were a prominent area along the Deerfield River.) The poem first appeared in George Sheldon's essay, "Negro Slavery in Old Deerfield" (1893).

But Hammon, of Queens Village, Long Island was probably the first person of African descent to publish a poem ("An Evening Thought: Salvation by Christ, with Penitential Cries . . . etc.") in English (1760), and Wheatley was the first to publish a collection of verse, *Poems on Various Subjects* (1773).

Both Wheatley and Hammon, slaves with "advantages and privileges"—as Hammon said of himself—were strongly influenced by the Wesley-Whitefield evangelist movement. They wrote the type of sentimental and pious Christian poetry typical of and favored by the Puritans in New England at that time—a point that Thomas Jefferson might have added to his comment about Wheatley's work being "below the dignity of criticism." Better educated than both Terry or Hammon, Wheatley's poems show—relatively speaking—a level of technical skill absent in their work.

The period between the 1820s to the end of the Civil War gave rise to black poets who spoke out—though perhaps not always strongly—against slavery. Many of them also looked piously to middle-class gentility, British verse, and European Christianity for models, and only mar-

ginally to their own culture and tradition. Poets such as Mary E. Tucker
Lambert, George Boyer Vashon, Ann Plato, James Monroe Whitfield,
Charles Lewis Reason, Carlotte L. Forten Grimke, Timothy Thomas
Fortune, Henrietta Allson Whitman, Alfred Isay Walden, and Elymas
Payson Rogers—all considered minor poets—at least to some extent,
showed only marginal interest in black folk material.

But then that tradition—the folk—had yet to gain in respectability. The richness and power of it were perhaps too close to be seen
clearly. Clergymen and professors, these poets wrote in formal religious terms and too often (like their white counterparts) were formally derivative. They *were* concerned with injustice and war, yes, and
spoke out against American hypocrisy, but most of them were also
much concerned with making a good impression—with, in effect,
proving that "colored" folks were intelligent enough to write verse in
the manner of the poets of England.

Then in 1829, George Moses Horton (1797?-1883?), sometimes
called "The Colored Bard of North Carolina," at about the age of
thirty-two, published his first collection, *The Hope of Liberty* (reprinted
in 1837 as *Poems by a Slave*), and in that volume we can see the beginnings of a black poet's efforts to break away from the earlier themes.
Like the authors of the slave narratives, he too spoke out against slavery, and is considered the first *southern* slave to do so in print.

But Paul Laurence Dunbar, the first major African American
poet, turned, for sustenance and for models, to the folk tradition more
dramatically than any previous poet of African descent. His poetry
reflects a wide range of ideas, forms, and habits in African American
folk culture. He made use of the spirituals, the storytelling tradition,
work songs, sermons, tall-tales, the secular and religious blues songs.
Yet Dunbar too was cautious about what his work implied and what
he said in print. Diplomatic and optimistic at the same time, his was a
careful militancy.

While Dunbar's African American contemporaries writing
poetry—James Weldon Johnson, Frances Ellen Watkins Harper,
James Edwin Campbell, Aaron Belford Thompson, Charles Douglas
Clem, Josephine D. Head, James D. Corrothers, James Ephriam
McGirth, William Stanley Braithwaite, Daniel Webster Davis,
Benjamin T. Tanner, Frank Barbour Coffin, Joseph Seamon Cotter, and

Alice Dunbar Nelson, to name a few—reflected some of the same thematic concerns, the same political caution, the same optimism, the same measured social militancy, none of them—with the possible exception of Johnson—equaled him in literary range and power.

While this was a period of accommodationist thinking, it was also the beginning of serious political and social protest. With this new-found confidence, African American poets, whether in terms of dialect or the King's English, began to explore their own folk culture. (Johnson's novel, *The Autobiography of an Ex-Colored Man* [1912], in a sense, is a romantic, if ironic, embracing of the folk tradition in that the protagonist recognizes and admires the richness of it but chooses to turn his back on it.) The embracing of the folk culture was a conscious choice on the part of the poets of this period.

And this conscious choice placed American black poetry firmly in the broadest and oldest context of world poetry—oral and musical—where it remains. As suggested earlier, poetry is, after all, a form of music made out of words. So, a written tradition, based on an oral one, evolved side by side with that continuing oral tradition. But African American literature, again formally speaking, did not evolve in this way in isolation. Its developmental pattern correlates with—while maintaining its own distinctive elements—the evolution of various forms of American writing generally.

Yet in this period following the Civil War, black poets (and writers of prose) interested in creating believable, true images of their people and the diverse experiences of those people, were up against a hard wall of public resistance. Remember, this was a time that gave rise to a popular generation of white American writers and poets—many politically to the right, pro-slavery, even reactionary—who worked in what we now call the Plantation Tradition. These writers—Joel Chandler Harris, Thomas Nelson Page, William John Grayson, Ruth McEnery Stuart, Irwin Russell, Sidney Lanier, and others—developed formulaic images of the ex-slave as buffoon, lazy roustabout, figure of ridicule, mammy, half-wit, criminal, thief, and rapist.

These minstrel and sentimental stereotypes were deeply implanted in the American psyche, not only by way of the stories and poems of these writers, but through the vastly popular traveling minstrel stage and sideshows and newspaper cartoons of the day. The legacy of those stereotypes, a hundred and thirty years later, is still with us—both in popular culture and to some extent in literature.

As the end of the nineteenth century approached, American writing generally—and African American writing in particular—showed signs of breaking away from its absolute dependency on European influences. Walt Whitman was also at work boldly creating and insisting on a *native* art form. The idea of a *formal* native poetry—though still a strange idea—was at least now in the vocabulary. True, even if he and those few who believed as he did didn't have a large tribe of followers.

During this period, Paul Laurence Dunbar's achievement in writing deceptively simple pastoral poetry matches Charles Waddell Chesnutt's in serious literary fiction and Du Bois's in lyrical analytical nonfiction. (By the way, in terms of form, Dunbar was influenced more by the poetry of Swinburne and Rossetti than by, say, Whitman or even Tennyson.)

Dunbar's dialect verse became better known than some of his more complex and sophisticated poems, of which there were many more and by which he is represented in this anthology. (Dunbar, among other early black poets, is the clear forerunner of the jazz poetry of the sixties, seventies, and eighties, and today's rap and hip-hop poetry.) In a way, it was William Dean Howells's introduction to Dunbar's first commercially published volume, *Lyrics of Lowly Life* (1896), that helped to bring a certain respectability to dialect poetry *by black poets.*

But neither the dialect nor the "straight" poetry earned him much money. He made a modest living, into the twentieth century, writing novels about white characters. Unlike the dialect poetry of white southern poets such as those mentioned a moment ago, Dunbar's is distinguished by its use of *readable* dialect and believable if not complex—and certainly likable!—characters. (This is not to say that some black poets didn't also write bad dialect poetry: James Edwin Campbell certainly did.)

An early Dunbar poem titled "Sympathy," which appears in *Oak and Ivy* (1893), shows—despite its somewhat insipid nature—the young poet's talent and ability to echo the dialect tradition, but a poem written near the end of that same decade (when Dunbar was not yet thirty and with less than ten years to live) and published under the same title, "Sympathy," is Dunbar at his best. The third stanza reads:

I know why the caged bird sings, ah me,
    When his wing is bruised and his bosom sore,—
When he beats his bars and he would be free;
It is not a carol of joy or glee,
    But a prayer that he sends from his heart's core,
But a plea, that upward to Heaven he flings—
I know why the caged bird sings!

The greatness of the poem is in its powerful rhythms and in its sophisticated use of sentiment to forge the startling and beautiful image of the caged bird without resorting to maudlin sentimentality.

During the first two decades of the twentieth century the so-called "New Negro" came into vogue, and for the first time the general public started reading the poetry and prose of African Americans. The Dunbar-Chesnutt-Du Bois-James Weldon Johnson generation of writers became the Old Guard as a group of younger poets—Claude McKay, Countee Cullen, Jean Toomer, Langston Hughes, and others—emerged as the leading poets of what later was called the Harlem Renaissance.

But who were these young upstarts? In terms of poetic form, they were individualistic, but in terms of thematic concerns they—especially Toomer, McKay, and Langston Hughes—shared a great deal.

Toomer's poem "Her Lips Are Copper Wire," for example, is an "imagistic" modernist work as vigorous and original as the best of its period:

> whisper of yellow globes
> gleaming on lamp-posts that sway
> like bootleg licker drinkers in the fog
>
> and let your breath be moist against me
> like bright beads on yellow globes
>
> telephone the power-house
> that the main wires are insulate
>
> (her words play softly up and down
> dewy corridors of billboards)

> then with your tongue remove the tape
> and press your lips to mine
> till they are incandescent

She is, of course, a work of art, one to behold. The poem is about
desire that follows a kiss. Here, electrical energy is compared to the
energy of the kiss, a kiss like electricity. (Copper wire was used to con-
duct electricity to the first electric streetlights.) The images of "bright
beads on yellow globes" and lampposts in a row form a kind of "cor-
ridor" and in the "dew" of night. They and everything else are shroud-
ed in a moist softness. Toomer's poem, like so much of his work, is a
celebration of life itself as he insists that energy equals life.

The new poetry was vigorous, and often universal in its subject
matter and themes, yet retained much of the sensitivity to racial issues
and injustice as expressed by the earlier generation. Modernism was in
the air, Ezra Pound, T. S. Eliot, e. e. cummings, Amy Lowell, and other
key white American poets of the period were self-consciously
involved in exploring new forms. They were all—black and white—
breathing the same air.

It is often said that Claude McKay's *Harlem Shadows* (1922) signaled the African American shift—at least in poetry—to the self-consciously modern mode, and, at the same time, the beginning of "The
New Negro" Movement, better known as the Harlem Renaissance.
But a McKay volume published two years earlier, *Spring in New
Hampshire and Other Poems,* reflects as much of the same consciousness
of the new aesthetic, which insisted that a poem was a lyrical *thing* and
not merely a vehicle for ideas.

Despite McKay's aesthetic sophistication as a poet, a considerable
number of contemporary critics believe that McKay's poetry lacks originality. On the contrary, McKay's best poetry is every bit as vibrant and
fresh as, say, Toomer's. Listen to McKay's "The Tropics in New York":

> Bananas ripe and green, and ginger-root,
> Cocoa in pods and alligator pears,
> And tangerines and mangoes and grape fruit,
> Fit for the highest prize at parish fairs,

Set in the window, bringing memories
Of fruit-trees laden by low-singing rills,
And dewy dawns, and mystical blue skies
In benediction over nun-like hills.

My eyes grew dim, and I could no more gaze;
A wave longing through my body swept,
And, hungry for the old, familiar ways,
I turned aside and bowed my head and wept.

The poem conjures up, in vivid images of the Caribbean, specifically Jamaica, the familiar paradox of being compelled to be far from one's beloved home, a paradox often expressed in McKay's work. The auto-biographical short story "Truant," *(Gingertown,* 1932) in part, deals with this subject in great detail. The paradox is not only based on the poet's nostalgic love for the green hills of Jamaica, juxtaposed with his attraction to the great steel and asphalt world of the city, but also on the struggle between the moral and social demands made by the city and the relative "freedom" suggested by the simpler way of life in a tropic setting.

In other words, and in a more subtle sense, the struggle for the poet is between life and art—and the hungry poet wants both. In an untitled poem in that same short story, McKay describes the cities of the northeastern United States "Where factories grow like jungle trees, / Yielding new harvest for the world." (p. 159) And McKay, in the prose text, continues the thought: "The steel-framed poetry of cities did not crowd out but rather intensified in him the singing memories of his village life." The point was, of course: "He loved both, the one complementing the other."

These poets, Jean Toomer, Langston Hughes, Claude McKay, and Arna Bontemps, in matters of technique and form, as I said before, aligned themselves with the modernist movement—as expressed by, say, William Carlos Williams. Like Williams, Hughes especially was interested in unearthing a native tongue, an American idiom, speaking his poetry in that tongue. This is Langston Hughes's poem "Cross" (1925):

My old man's a white old man
And my old mother's black.

> If ever I cursed my white old man
> I take my curses back.
>
> If ever I cursed my black old mother
> And wished she were in hell,
> I'm sorry for that evil wish
> And now I wish her well.
>
> My old man died in a fine big house.
> My ma died in a shack.
> I wonder where I'm gonna die,
> Being neither white nor black?

The poem achieves its "sonic" power and complexity through repetition of certain words: "old," "man," "curse," "black," "white," "shack," "hell," and "well."

Thematically on one level about anger and forgiveness, on another it ultimately explores a full network of profound social and philosophical issues. Each quatrain, for example, advances the racial paradox of a complex fate, especially when one considers the social context in which the dilemma occurs: a racist society. This social context operates here as a subtext. In certain other cultures and to varying degrees, the so-called racial "color" aspects might cause bewilderment, but in terms of the class issues raised by the speaker, the poem would be understood universally. Each of us, it seems to say, has some type of "cross" to bear. "Color" as it relates to a mixed race person's identity is an issue, yes, but coupled with it, inseparable from it, is the equally urgent issue of mortality: "I wonder where I'm gonna die."

Many of the other prominent black poets of this period—especially Countee Cullen and James Weldon Johnson—were largely influenced by the conservative technical tradition (sometimes called the academic tradition) handed down in British verse by Shelley, Byron, and Keats, and carried on (and also then newly redefined, incidentally) by such white American poets as Allen Tate.

Cullen's "ear" for the music of the language was as good as the best. This is the opening couplet from "Leaves":

> One, two and three,
> Dead leaves drift from a tree.

Despite the fact that he paid little attention to the American idiom, and held fast to the European Romantic tradition of poetic language to the point of being a bit out of step at best and old fashioned at worst, Cullen has to be seen as a serious poet of considerable accomplishments in this period called the Harlem Renaissance.

In a way, Bontemps, though, might be closer to another kind of modernist, Wallace Stevens, than to Williams Carlos Williams, in that he was interested in looking deeply into the meaning of life and making complex philosophical connections. Never fully appreciated as a poet by the reading public, Bontemps, in my opinion, was a poet of great breadth and depth who has been denied credit for his brilliant accomplishments. In the first stanza of his visionary "Close Your Eyes," listen to the sharp, clear voice, see the dramatically etched image of the idealized landscape, the gate, the woodman, the hill:

> Go through the gates with closed eyes.
> Stand erect and let your black face front the west.
> Drop the axe and leave the timber where it lies;
> a woodman on the hill must have his rest.

That this modernist movement carried the name Harlem in its title was of course only symbolic, and, as many have suggested, maybe even natural, because New York City was and is perhaps the greatest artistic and cultural center in the States. In his introduction to *The New Negro* (1968), Alain Locke—a professor at Howard University in Washington D.C., and an important historical scholar of the movement—attempted to refocus the "New Negro" in the quickly evolving context of the modern world taking shape after the first world war. He said:

> . . . the New Negro must be seen in the perspective of a
> New World, and especially of a New America. Europe
> seething in a dozen centers with emergent nationalities,
> Palestine full of a renascent Judaism—these are no more
> alive with the progressive forces of our era than the quick-

ened centers of the lives of black folk. America seeking a new spiritual expansion and artistic maturity, trying to found an American literature, a national art, and national music implies a Negro-American culture seeking the same satisfactions and objectives. Separate as it may be in color and substance, the culture of the Negro is of a pattern integral with the times and with its cultural setting.

Locke went on to say that "Negro life" was "finding a new soul. There is a fresh spiritual and cultural focusing." He saw a renewal of "race-spirit" and great creativity that "proudly sets itself apart." He called what he saw "the Negro Renaissance."

Then in 1929 publishers and other supporters of the movement, with tight budgets resulting from the world economic crisis, turned away. The public attention given the Harlem Renaissance started winding down from that point on. By the mid-thirties many of the poets (fiction writers, painters, sculptors, playwrights, actors, musicians, and other artists associated with the movement) were starved for attention.

In African American literature, the period between the late thirties and the early sixties, sometimes called the "protest" period, which correlated with hard times in America, is best known for its black prose writers such as Richard Wright, Chester Himes, Ann Petry, Dorothy West, Ralph Ellison, and later, James Baldwin. But, as quiet as it was and still is kept, some of the finest black poets—Gwendolyn Brooks, Margaret Walker, Sterling Brown, Robert Hayden—the culture had produced up till that point were at work. These poets were users of the folk culture in either rural or urban settings.

Take Gwendolyn Brooks. Using a modernist aesthetic, and in poems variously about racism, sexism, and classism, Brooks has explored social problems, poverty, social justice, black rage, and pain. Her setting has often been Chicago's South Side—in the forties known as the Black Belt or Black Metropolis. Brooks called it Bronzeville, and focused on the relationship between the individual and the community. In graceful line after graceful line, in a powerful performative voice, she took the reader into bleak kitchenettes and into the crowded streets. From "Kitchenette Building":

We are things of dry hours and the involuntary plan,
Grayed in, and gray . . .

But her work has always been about a great deal more—about love, about
other locations. The first six lines of "Strong Men, Riding Horses":

Strong Men, riding horses. In the West
On a range five hundred miles. A Thousand. Reaching
From dawn to sunset. Rested blue to orange.
From a hope to crying. Except that Strong Men are
Desert-eyed. Except that Strong Men are
Pasted to stars already . . .

The poem relies on an interplay of sound and color that evokes powerful images of a way of life vastly different from that lived by most people on the South Side of Chicago, as the rest of the poem demonstrates.

While Gwendolyn Brooks explored primarily African American
urban folk culture, Sterling A. Brown, using the folk idiom or rural
black speech, investigated the rural culture and the possibilities of
dialect poetry. An expert in the folklore of his culture, Brown was
interested in the so-called "low-down" people and found the
Depression years a ripe source of subject matter. He believed in what
was then called "the common man." The models for his poems were
the work songs, the blues, the spirituals. Among his many themes were
the early-twentieth-century relationship between the town and the
city, the effect of the railroad on individual and community life, the
interplay between black people and white people, and so on. This is
the first stanza of "Foreclosure":

Father Missouri takes his own.
These are the fields he loaned them,
Out of heart's fullness, gratuitously;
Here are the banks he built up for his children,
Here are the fields, rich fertile silt.

Consider Hayden, too, for example. Hayden, without question, is
a major American poet whose gift is large and whose understanding

of the craft matches that of, say, Bud Powell in jazz, Romare Bearden in painting. This is from "Names":

> Once they were sticks and stones
> I feared would break my bones:
> Four Eyes. And worse.
> Old Four Eyes fled
> to safety in the danger zones
> Tom Swift and Kubla Khan traversed.

Here, the poet looks back at the "names" he was called as a child, revisits the pain caused by the cruelty of other children, and remembers retreating into the "safety in the danger zones" of books, the magical world of literature.

We tend to associate poets with the periods in which they came into prominence, and in a way that is often unfair. Such poets as Arna Bontemps and Langston Hughes were still writing and producing some of their best works, and, in fact, reinventing their public personas through these works, in the new contexts of the fifties and sixties.

Then there are really fine poets not as widely known who have worked for several decades—from the fifties through the eighties and longer—such as Pinkie Gordon Lane, Norman Henry Pritchard II, Lebert Bethune, Ed Roberson, Conyus, Russell Atkins, and Gloria Oden, to name just a few, without proper recognition. This is the first stanza of Oden's "The Carousel":

> An empty carousel in a deserted park
> rides me round and round,
> from end to beginning,
> like the tail that drives the dog.

There is no way to miss the beauty and energy of such an image. It comes at you full force.

Pritchard and Atkins, on the other hand, occupy a special place in the ranks of African American poets working in the sixties and seventies. Both might be described as "concrete" poets, but that word doesn't really do them justice. You could just as well call them "cubist" poets. I think of Bach when I read Atkins. I think of early Picasso when I read Pritchard. The point is, they make the presence of the poem on the page as significant as the poem's meanings and sounds. This is Atkins's "Probability and Birds in the Yard":

> The probability in the yard is this:
> The rodent keeps the cat close by;
> The cat would sharp the bird;
> the bird would waft to the water—
> if he does he has but his times before,
> whichever one he is. He's surely marked.
>
> The cat is variable;
> the rodent becomes the death of the bird
> which we love
>   dogs are random

And Pritchard, like an abstract expressionist at times, like a cubist at other times: this is "Burnt Sienna":

> Trust thrust first tinder kindling grown
> the maple gave rust air its bark
> and ample and plain
> fair orange orb
> sworn to that sea line stretching bare
> courteous and neat
> still gleaming meekly weaned
> by some awesome twilight rise
> beyond be gone
> the nameless coloured yarn

But it was not till the sixties, during the Civil Rights Movement, that the general poetry-reading public—sparked by the loud clamor of many people fighting for freedom from racism, sexism, war, for justice—started reading and listening to African American poetry again. Poets born in the thirties had come of age—Derek Walcott, Etheridge

Knight, Gerald Barrax, Audre Lorde, Sonia Sanchez, Jay Wright, Colleen J. McElroy, Jayne Cortez, Norman Henry Pritchard II, Ed Roberson, Amiri Baraka, and others of the period tried to give lyrical expression to the complex personal, social, and political issues before them.

This is Baraka (when he was still LeRoi Jones) at his best with "For Hettie":

> My Wife is left-handed.
> Which implies a fierce de-
> termination. A complete other
> worldliness. IT'S WEIRD BABY
> The way some folks
> are always trying to be different.
>
> But then, she's been a bohemian
> all her life . . . black stockings,
> refusing to take orders. I sit
> patiently, trying to tell her
> what's right. TAKE THAT DAMN
> PENCIL OUTTA THAT HAND. YOU'RE
> RITING BACKWARDS. & such. But
> to no avail. & it shows
> in her work. Left-handed coffee
> left-handed eggs: when she comes
> in at night . . . it's her left hand
> offered for me to kiss. DAMN.
>
> & now her belly droops over the seat.
> They say it's a child. But
> I ain't quite so sure.

This is a love poem sung by a man in love with his wife in her ninth month, in love with her for her "fierce determination." The baby is late. The wonderfully and playfully sardonic tone is fresh, immediate, and refreshing. Left-handedness here is a metaphor for the wife's rebellion against convention. She's "a bohemian," she's even planning natural childbirth at a time—the fifties—when it was rare in the States. Hettie

Jones, LeRoi Jones's first wife, in her autobiography *How I Became Hettie Jones* (1990), says, "What I prized in myself he loved most."

These were the days when poets started singing and chanting their poetry before audiences, putting it on record. In an article of mine, called "The Explosion of Black Poetry," which appeared in *Essence* as the sixties pushed into the early seventies, I tried to map some of this excitement, calling it "a great explosion." Rap, in a sense, has been one outgrowth of that explosion.

From the late seventies through the mid-nineties, African American poetry—along with American poetry generally—despite the conservative political climate, continued to regain its good health. New voices of poets born in the forties—Ellease Southerland, Quincy Troupe, Sherley Anne Williams, Calvin Forbes, Marilyn Nelson Waniek, Nathaniel Mackey, Christoper Gilbert, and others— emerged or gained prominence for the first time. A richness and universality of theme and technical maturity were present in much of the work. Waniek, for example, was not afraid to explore the much treaded territory of the traditional ballad, and to come up with refreshing results. Here is the opening quatrain of "The Ballad of Aunt Geneva":

> Geneva was the wild one.
> Geneva was a tart.
> Geneva met a blue-eyed boy
> and gave away her heart.

It was as though the new generation had learned from the mistakes of excessive didacticism of many of those who came of age in the sixties and early seventies. This is an another example—the opening lines of Christopher Gilbert's "Kite-flying":

> June at Truro Beach the joyous bathers,
> specks of jewel fallen along the sand.
> Walking near them there is this polarity—
> their lives the way stars hold the sky . . .

Adding the younger poets of this period—Lucinda Roy, Karen
Mitchell, Michael S. Weaver, Cornelius Eady, Patricia Smith, Lenard D.
Moore, Carl Phillips, Thomas Sayers Ellis, Elizabeth Alexander, Kevin
Young, C. S. Giscombe, and others—to the list makes the nineties look
like another renaissance, one bolstered by the proliferation of tech-
nology into an outburst of diverse creativity many times greater than
that first one in the twenties.

A couple of examples of their voices:

C. S. Giscombe's cryptic "note-taking" style—echoing Paul
Blackburn, Gary Snyder, and Robert Creeley in some ways—is concise,
unpredictable, odd and, at times, vividly beautiful: lines from "(1980)":

> In the dream I became 2 men my age
> & we confronted the old man
> > who'd been K's lover once who
> > wanted her back he sd
> on whose land she still lived

> but that one of us was black, the other "of mixed blood"

Such lines move as intricately woven patterns, indeed, just like the candid language of risky dreams, moving from the emotional depths of the
most private places to places postpersonal yet not quite public, making
the journey with elegance and urgency as they attempt to render a
hard-won "self," in line-by-line breath, with no frills.

Three lines from "Suffering the Sea Change: All My Pretty
Ones," by Lucinda Roy:

> What isn't water in us must be bone;
> what isn't weeping must be what remains
> when weeping's done.

Three lines of precision, intensity, understanding, power, and beauty.

Giscombe's, Roy's and the other voices of this newest generation
of poets are as individual and as rooted in the culture as I imagine it's
possible to be in this day and age of internationalism and multicultur-
alism. Their voices are constructed out of intense cultural and artistic

conflict and cross-fertilization. This, for example, is Michael S. Weaver's
last stanza in "My Father's Geography":

> *At a phone looking to Africa over the Mediterranean,*
> *I called my father, and, missing me, he said,*
> *"You almost home boy. Go on cross that sea!"*

"Go on cross that sea," indeed.

In African American poetry, there were many seas to cross and there
are many seas yet to cross—most of them at home, on these shores. In
1931 James Weldon Johnson wrote a new preface to his 1922 classic
anthology *The Book of American Negro Poetry*. Near the end of that
introduction Johnson said, "I do not wish to be understood to hold
any theory that they [Negro poets] should limit themselves to Negro
themes; the sooner they are able to write American poetry sponta-
neously, the better." (p. 42) That, as it turns out, is a domestic "sea"
African American poets have now clearly crossed.

At the end of Johnson's long preface he said: "Much ground has
been covered, but more will yet be covered. It is this side of prophecy
to declare that the undeniable creative genius of the Negro is destined
to make a distinctive and valuable contribution to American poetry."

RHYTHM: TALKING THAT TALK

My interest in informal speech is long-standing. I edited two dictionaries of African American "slang," an antidotal one in 1970, and a scholarly one in 1994. The latter was not an embellishment of the earlier one. The interest stems from two concerns: one, for the richness and the way informal speech nourishes formal speech, and two, for the ways I could possibly use that richness in my own writing.

Slang has never had a consistently good reputation. Often it is characterized as much by arrogance, bigotry, sexism, and self-contempt as by humor, compassion, and wisdom. But it also happens to be the most alive aspect of our language. My goal, at least in part, was to help bring to the language we call slang a better name, a better reputation; and also to suggest, by the example of those dictionaries, how intrinsic it is to the quest of human culture to express and to renew itself.

Also, there is the sense that slang is tolerated because, for the most part (in the minds of some critics), it belongs to the young, the youth culture, and there is the sense, or hope, that they will eventually grow out of it, advance to standard speech, which, the official guardians of the culture seem to hope, will signal their acceptance of the status quo. J. L. Dillard makes the point in *Lexicon of Black English* (1977), that the word *slang* itself has caused many people to take lightly or negatively a complex and rich language.

> The general public has long associated slang with a transitory stage in the language development of teenagers, soon to be dropped by all except those few who never enter the

adult, mainstream world. "Slang" was, for the average
American, an exotic language phenomenon primarily for
children outside the domain of working language and not
really to be considered seriously. (p. 17)

Kids aside, maybe the case is more pervasive and serious than that.
Slang has always been considered, by official watchers of culture, to be
a threat to not only "proper" language but to "proper" society as well.
Irving Lewis Allen, in his *City in Slang: New York Life and Popular
Speech* (1993), takes a broader view:

> Around 1850 the word slang, while in English a century
> earlier, became the accepted term for "illegitimate" and
> other unconventional speech. Disapproving comment on
> low speech forms, fueled by class anxieties in the chang-
> ing city, probably helped establish the word slang in the
> United States. By 1900 the term had all its present mean-
> ings, including that of a vocabulary regarded as below
> standard and that threatened proper, genteel usages. . . .
> Street speech . . . expressed the troublesome spirit of the
> social underside of the industrial city: unconventional,
> experimental without license, insubordinate, scornful of—
> or merely careless of—authority. These locutions spread
> rapidly and began to be noticed, recorded, and deemed
> something of a social problem. (pp. 22-23)

The way black jazz and blues musicians have been talking, say, since
the latter part of the nineteenth century, might be seen as an outstanding example of this rebellion Allen speaks of. In fact, Robert S.
Gold, in his introduction to *A Jazz Lexicon* (1964), supports Allen's
claim, saying that there is an "essential rebelliousness at the heart of
both the music and the speech" (xviii). And I would go so far as to say
that *all* alive art is rebellious, and *all* alive speech, slang or otherwise, is
rebellious, rebellious in the healthy sense that they challenge the stale
and the conventional.

African American slang cuts through logic and arrives at a quick,
efficient, interpretative solution to situations and things otherwise

difficult to articulate. It serves as a device for articulating every conceivable thing imaginable—the nature of sex, the taste of food, social relationships, life itself, and death. Just as the word "Watergate" explains a vast and complex incident, a word like "bondage," to refer to being "in debt," or a phrase like "jump the broom," to explain that somebody will get married, makes the point quickly with a strong, clear, symbolic gesture, and a sense of vibrant, alive humor.

Black slang is a living, breathing form of expression that changes so quickly no researcher can keep up with it. A word or phrase can come into existence to mean one thing among a limited number of speakers in a particular neighborhood and a block away it might mean something else or be unknown entirely—at least for a while.

One group of speakers—such as a gang, a social club, or even a whole neighborhood—may feel the need for secrecy from another gang, social club, or neighborhood only just around the corner. At this point, when it is most private, this mode of speech thrives and is at its most effective. It is the classic example of a secret tongue. At the same time, both groups will feel the need to maintain a rapidly changing vocabulary unknown to the larger, mainstream culture, known generally or loosely as white America. The need for secrecy is part of the reason for the rapid change.

Since the days of slavery, this secrecy has served as a form of cultural self-defense against exploitation and oppression, constructed out of a combination of language, gesture, body style, and facial expression. In its embryonic stages during slavery, the secrecy was a powerful medium for making sense out of a cruel and strange world. African American slang is a kind of "home talk" in the sense that it was not originally meant for listeners beyond the nest.

As is always the case with informal private talk, it becomes, formally speaking, *informal* language—slang—when it reaches the larger speaking population. In other words, slang is, in a sense, a corruption of the more private forms of informal speech, such as cant, argot, or jargon. This evolution from private to public is natural for the words and phrases strong enough to survive for any considerable length of time.

But once such a transition is made, original meanings are very often lost. For example, "uptight" in the fifties, among the original group of black speakers who created the term, had a specific sexual reference. Once the phrase fell into general use, it took on a psychological meaning, referring to some sort of mental disturbance. This evolution from private to public is not only essential to the vitality at the crux of slang, but inevitable. By this I mean, African American slang is not only a living language for black speakers but for the whole country, as evidenced by its popularity decade after decade since the beginning of American history. The most recent example of this popularity is rap and hip-hop during the 1980s and the 1990s.

One important aspect of this "aliveness" is its onomatopoeic tendency. How words sound has always interested black speakers. Zap, yacky-de-yack, bop, bebop, ticktock, O-bop-she-bam, hoochy-coochy, honkytonk—all have been popular at one time or another. Perhaps even more than any other type of slang words, onomatopoeic words deliver the pleasure of immediacy—the "sock!" (as in "sock it to me").

In a similar way, the rhyming jargon of black slang gives the same sort of satisfaction—especially for the pleasures of syncopated sound—as do rhyming terms such as Muhammad Ali's "rope-a-dope." Related in form is the language of rap and hip-hop. Rappers and would-be rappers carry on a tradition—just as the break dancing of the eighties followed the flash dancing of the forties—that started with pre-twentieth-century forms of playful, informal African American speech.

Some rap and hip-hop words and phrases will enter the canon, just as in the past hip and jive words such as "dude" and "cool" ended up in general use and in dictionaries.

While a certain vocabulary or idiom might please and serve one decade or generation, it will not necessarily work for the next. Changes in black slang word forms take place continually. It happens when speakers drop syllables, usually from the end or sometimes from the beginning of a word, such as "Bama" for Alabama, "cap" for "backcap," "bam" for "bambita," "bro" for "brother," or "head" for "crackhead."

Other changes occur through shifts in the function of African American slang words. A noun, for example, might be used as a verb: "He *boozed* himself to death" or "I *jived* my way to Brooklyn." Black speech is fluid in this way because it remains open to the influences of verbal forces from every conceivable direction.

And it is important to remember that it is anonymous speakers who create and sustain the initial contents and shape of this language. Black social groups across the country are the homes of such anonymous speakers. Their talk draws on many levels of language, and popular culture in general, for its storehouse of words and phrases.

Let me return to an earlier point in order to complete the thought. The private talk of an African American gang or social club becomes slang when it reaches the larger African American community or communities. It continues to be slang from that point on as it moves out into the general American speaking public. But African American slang is *not* colloquialism; it is not dialect, not argot, not jargon or cant. Black slang is composed of or involves the use of redundancies, jive rhyme, nonsense, fad expressions, nicknames, corruptions, onomatopoeia, mispronunciations, and clipped forms.

In this way, the collective verbal force of black speakers throughout the many black communities in America carries on the tradition of renewing the American language while resisting and using it. Yet African American informal speech and slang are quite distinct in many essential ways from common American speech and slang. There is a basic grammatical difference between black speech and American English. Today, in the 1990s, nouns, for example, tend to be repeated within a single sentence along with pronouns as they were 150 years ago. At the same time, the overall shape of African American slang is also influenced, through exchange and conflict, by American English words and phrases that are adjusted to the African forms.

Again, for example, "This guy, he come at me out of nowhere." Or, "The mayor, he done the best he could with an impossible situation." Past, present, and future tenses are often not used in the expected order. No matter the subject, it gets the same verb form. Plurals are employed where in English structure they are not required. Sentences are commonly structured without the "to be" verb forms.

To say it another way, what I am calling African American slang *includes* black dialect, but slang and idiom are not the same thing as dialect. Black speakers generally sound like other speakers of their regions. We know this as dialect. But African American slang, as late as the 1920s, 1930s, and 1940s, was still largely regionalized. If, in the thirties, a southern black speaker of slang came into contact with a northern black speaker of slang, neither one usually had any idea what the other was talking about.

Today, in the nineties, just about every segment of the country is in touch with every other, due to television and radio, air travel and telephones, faxes and computers, so a homogenized form of African American slang has been emerging since the 1950s while dialects seem less altered by extra-regional influences.

This makes for a fertile language environment and for even more accelerated change in African American slang. It evolved over the decades best when the social and political atmospheres were most fluid and creative. A social environment that is accommodating is necessary for the evolution of any form of slang. African American communities have been generally receptive to slang, although it has had to evolve in a moral war zone between the secular position of street culture and the sacred position of the sisters and deacons of the black church.

American society generally is receptive to slang. Slang never evolves in isolation. Black slang in particular uses the receptive American atmosphere to its own advantage while creating and maintaining a private language with its own center of gravity, integrity, and shape.

Many of the words and phrases are borrowed from very specific cultural pockets in the country—from the drug scene, prison life, street life, entertainment, and especially the areas of blues and jazz. These categories are important areas upon which black slang draws. They are every bit as essential to the vitality of black slang as is the presence of the mainstream American cultural scene.

This also means that, even when there is relatively little direct outside contact or communication between African Americans and other American social and racial subgroups, cross-fertilization—by way of television or whatever—is essential for the continuation of a private black alternative language—one that is, to some extent, destined to return to the white public arena from which it was borrowed.

So it is useless to ask, "Why an alternative language? Why not *one* American tongue for every ethnic or social group?" Most African Americans, like most Americans of any ethnic group, are skilled in what is called the common American culture—and the American language is the instrument of that culture. Each group's individual cultural identity is essentially established through the bond of its own distinctive expression. As is the case for other subcultures, African Americans are *also* skilled in their own racial culture. Informal speech is part of that culture, and they have many effective uses for informal speech. In daily life there are situations so sensitive or painful that slang often seems the only way to deal with them.

One of the primary functions of this language is its quest to create a coherent cultural construct of positive self-images. Though many of the words and phrases may sound harsh and even obscene to outsiders, the language is essential to the cultural enrichment of African Americans.

Black speakers, in self-mockery, can call each other "nigger" and, in a sense, make null and void racial slurs of white bigots. As James Baldwin often said, "I told you *first.*" But the effectiveness of such a strategy, and its long-term psychological benefits, remains open to question. Yet it is a social phenomenon that has significant historical consensus simply by virtue of its long practice.

American English, perhaps more than any other language, has borrowed from other tongues, period. Black slang is a form of black speech and black speech is a form of American English, but in the early stages, say, in the sixteenth century, black speech was still close to its African roots. Such African words and phrases as "okra," "cocacola," "turnip," "jazz," "gorilla," "banana," and "juke" (as in "jukebox"), for example, became common symbols in American English. More important, African American speech and slang have contributed to the ultimate formation of formal American English. And not only through the process of African nonslang words entering the language, but also as slang words and phrases such as "ace boon coon," "Afro," "attitude," "bad," "not," and so on, enter the mainstream formal language. Stuart Berg Flexner, in *I Hear America Talking* (1976), says:

> When we heard America talking, we heard Blacks talking
> . . . The "we" is Black and White. . . . The Blacks have
> influenced the American language in two major ways (1) by
> using many of their native (Black African) words and speech,
> and (2) by causing, doing, being, influencing things that have

had all America talking, often using terms created or popularized by the Black presence and expedience. (p. 31)

There are roughly four areas of African American slang: (1) the
early southern rural slang that started during slavery, (2) the slang of
the sinner-man/black musician of the period between 1900 and 1960,
(3) street culture slang out of which rap and hip-hop evolved, and (4)
working class slang. All areas are fully represented in this dictionary,
from the beginnings of black people in this country to the present.

The point, of course—and it's a pity to have to stress it—is that
not all black speech is "street speech." But a surprisingly large number
of Americans believe this to be so. "There are now thousands, perhaps
millions, of black Americans who . . . have limited contact with ver-
nacular black speech," says John Baugh in *Black Street Speech* (1983).
"Dialect boundaries therefore don't automatically conform to racial
groups. Then collectively, black Americans speak a wide range of
dialects, including impeccable standard English" (p. 127).

Not only has there been, historically speaking, geographically
determined diversity to African American slang, but the Africans who
made up the language out of Portuguese Pidgin, Bantu, and Swahili,
primarily, created what was known early on as Plantation Creole. The
persistence of Africanisms in the formation of black slang and African
American culture generally can be seen as a grand testimony to the
strength of the human spirit and to the cultural strength of that poly-
glot group of Africans dumped, starting in 1619, on this continent to
work the land.

But make no mistake, this is not another African language. And I
am not pushing an Afrocentric program by spelling out the origins of
this language. Black slang is an American language with distant roots
in the ancient coastal tribes of central west Africa, as well as, indirect-
ly, in Anglo-Irish culture and elsewhere.

But perhaps more important than any of the above is this: African
American speech and slang form is, in a sense, one of the primary cut-
ting edges against which American speech—formal and informal—
generally keeps itself alive.

CLAUDE MCKAY: MY 1975 ADVENTURE

Claude McKay was born in 1889 in Jamaica and died in 1948 in Chicago. At the time of his death, all ten of his books were out of print. Author of three novels, four books of poems, a collection of short stories, and an autobiography, McKay grew up in rural Jamaica, lived most of his short life in the United States, Europe, and North Africa, in bleak poverty, and died in extreme poverty and ill health. During the worst years of the Depression, McKay was forced to live in an upstate New York shelter for drunks and bums.

Another irony: McKay, better known as a poet, was by far a better novelist. Though it was in the United States that McKay published his books, he was not an American novelist. He was not an English writer, either, though some of his books were printed there. McKay was unquestionably an international writer. Two of his books were translated into Russian during his lifetime but none of his works have been published in his homeland. According to his friend and agent, Carl Cowl, McKay was never fully accepted in Jamaica. And he certainly was not really *involved* in the so-called Harlem Renaissance. It is simply another irony that his book, *Spring in New Hampshire and Other Poems* (1920) should be seen as the thing that kicked off the Harlem Renaissance.

Lately I've given a lot of thought to McKay. I was recently asked to write an introduction to three unpublished McKay manuscripts. They were to be published, but before I could finish my introduction, the project folded. The manuscripts (controlled by Hope McKay Virtue, McKay's daughter, and by Carl Cowl) went, I assume, to another publisher. This was mid-1974. I was left with a pile of notes.

I had reread all of McKay's poems and novels and Wayne Cooper's *The Passion of Claude McKay* (1973). It's the best book ever done on McKay. I met with Carl Cowl, a pleasantly intelligent man, and with Wayne Cooper, a brilliant scholar, somewhat shy, a white Southerner living in a Black neighborhood in Brooklyn. Cooper was doing some sort of night work in a hospital. His ambition was to collect and publish McKay's letters but he could not afford to work steadily on the project. Cooper also planned a full-scale biography of the Jamaican writer. I asked him about the possibility of his receiving a grant to hold him while doing his work. He smiled. Apparently he did not know the right people. My talks with Cowl and Cooper gave me insights and sidelights I would not have otherwise gained.

McKay is probably best known for his poem, "If We Must Die," which Winston Churchill recited at a crucial moment during the war. But *Banana Bottom* (1933), a novel, is McKay's best work. It is set in Jamaica and of his completed fiction, it is the most clearly conceived and imaginatively written. The pace is slow and, like many good books, it is not easy to read.

Yet I wonder about a McKay novel we will never see. He called it *Color Scheme.* William Bardly, his agent at the time, 1925, could not sell it because it was too frankly sexual. In a letter to A.A. Schomburg (quoted by Cooper in *Passion,* p.26), McKay says of *Color Scheme,* "I make my Negro characters yarn and backbite and fuck like people the world over." McKay eventually destroyed this, his first novel.

Identified as a writer of the so-called "low life," McKay wrote about prostitutes and pimps, pullman car porters, dreamers, revolutionaries, bums, drifters, cabaret good-time folks. Most of these characters were either at odds with or struggling against the concepts of the worlds in which they found themselves.

Stylistically, McKay was no innovator. His poetry was formal and rigidly conventional. His fictional technique showed the influence of more interesting concepts then being explored by D. H. Lawrence, Gertrude Stein, and several French writers of the 1920s. McKay's characters generally felt it better to live a carefree, gutsy, primitive life than to conform; better than to spend one's time a slave to the socially acceptable.

This is demonstrated dramatically in *Romance in Marseilles,* (1929–30), one of the unpublished McKay manuscripts. *Romance* is a thin, colorful, and choppy story of a West African black man who has just lost both legs and an Egyptian girl whoring on Marseilles's Quayside or, as McKay says, the Dreamport. It is the Mediterranean Harbor.

As the novel opens we see Lafala briefly in a New York hospital where his legs are being amputated. A crooked lawyer, called the Black Angel, handles Lafala's lawsuit against the shipping company which Lafala is suing for compensation. His position is simple: the company is responsible since ship authorities, after finding Lafala and his pal, Babel, aboard as stowaways, locked them in a place where Lafala's legs froze and therefore had to be taken off. Lafala is fixed up with artificial legs, the court rules in his favor, and he returns, this time as a ticket paying passenger, to Mediterranean Harbor, where he immediately begins to flaunt his potential settlement wealth. But the fifty thousand dollars is still a long way from his hands.

Right away two whores, Aslima and La Fleur Noire, start vying for his attention. La Fleur Noire doesn't stand a chance because Lafala already has his eyes set on Aslima. The "two wenches" fight like "little rats in the hole." Much of the battle takes place at the rendezvous of the colored colony, Cafe Tout-va-Bien. Rock, an American Black, Diup, a Senegalese, Petit Frère, who works at the Domino Cafe, and Big Blond, a white American (involved homosexually with Petit Frere), are a few of the characters who enter along the sidelines among a dazzling spread of love and drink seekers, drifters and dreamers, pimps and their women, revolutionaries and underdogs. Mostly they dance, fight, laugh, stretch out in the sun, maybe unload a ship for a little extra money with which to buy more Italian Spumanti. Etienne St. Dominique is the local crusader fighting for the rights of the Quayside dwellers.

With a belly full of wine and a light head, Lafala concludes that money is better than sound feet. Plus he is finally sleeping with the girl of his greatest daydream. In fact, he wants to marry her and take her with him to his homeland. Meanwhile, Titian, Aslima's evil-spirited pimp, is growing impatient and is not fully convinced that

Aslima is simply holding out for larger gains. Aslima continues to refuse the money that Lafala offers her. Theoretically, she is waiting for the full settlement. She permits Lafala to assume she is with him because she has sincere feelings for him. Cat Row is buzzing with gossip. Lafala plays the flute and remembers dancing the Banana-Split and the Jolly Pig.

Aslima's past rushes into the present. Born a slave in Marrakesh and raised in Moulay Abdallah by "a wise old courtesan," Aslima knows instinctively that Lafala, the cautious one, does not trust her though he wants her. She is waiting to gain his trust as well.

Before Lafala can get his hands on the settlement money, he and Babel are thrown in jail for the offense of stowing away. St. Dominique pulls a few powerful strings and the two pals are set free. Lafala's money is also now clear. Quayside jumps with joy. Folks are dancing and celebrating in the streets. McKay tells us there is a new feeling about and among Blacks.

Aslima plans to exploit and abandon Lafala. She also plans to stay with him. Titian resolves her conflict: he kills her.

Thematically and even structurally, *Romance* resembles *Banjo* (1929) minus the intellectual agonizing on political and social matters.

Lafala is based on a real person named Deda. McKay describes him in a letter (in the James Weldon Johnson Collection at Yale) dated January 13, 1928. Deda had been a great dancer much admired by the girls of Vreux Port quarters.

Harlem Glory, the second manuscript, is also a novel. Set in the early 1930s, its central figure is Buster South, a West Indian who lives in Harlem where he divides his time between running numbers, romancing women, and spiritualism. The story opens with Buster in Paris as Policy Queen Millinda Rose's traveling companion. There is a big party at Millinda's. Her secret is she's bankrupt—suddenly. She's the widow of the late, powerful Policy King Red Rose. Before the party ends, Millinda goes to the bathroom and commits suicide. And Buster returns to Harlem alone.

High life on Sugar Hill and the numbers racket seem to be in trouble. Not enough money around. Harlem big shots think that Whites—who have most of the money—should be spending more of it in Harlem. Because Buster knows how to deal with Whites and how to manipulate Blacks, he is considered valuable to the community. This is only one ideological force at work. There are others.

McKay fills the novel with many characters and aspects of Paris and Harlem life. There's a flashback to Red and Millinda's wedding on Sugar Hill; barbershop talk on man-woman relations; the relation of conjure and voodoo to the numbers and how the racket got started; the reader meets, in Paris, impish, light-skinned Lotta Sander; Baron Belchite, from Austria; Prince (black) and Princess (white) Kwakoh Fanti, from West Africa; pushy, middle-class, Afro-american Miss Aschine Palma; Madame Marie Audacem, a high society type; and others.

In Harlem, the impressionistic vision is just as wide. We hear Cleopatra Price testifying; witness Abdul, the revolutionary who dies in the end; we hear Katie, a maid, tell her story; Javan Brown loses his wife to the Glory Savior; Luther Sharpage is the Glory Savior's partner in the formation of the Helping Hand; we get a glimpse into the semi-secret spiritualist chapels of the Glory Soulers, a place of primitive Christian mysticism and African black magic and fetishism; we hear an alarming (and alarmed!) number of male characters referring to something called "the female problem"; there's Larry, the truck driver who goes wild from drinking rubbing alcohol; Baldwin Hatcher, the white journalist and radio personality; Tillie Ashmead, a teacher; Patsinette Smythe, a house decorator; Bibba Prentice, a numbers game controller; Millinda's cook, Charlotte and Charlotte's husband, Mr. Pointer; on the streets we see leather-coated dudes bopping and twitching in strange ways from the effects of reefer.

McKay takes us into a nickelodeon; we watch people sip hooch and read *The Harlem Nugget;* there's the Big Bang Club on 133rd between Fifth and Lexington; early on the reader meets the Senegalese dancer, Kamassa, and the Afro-american pianist, Pucksur, at Lamour's Cabaret playing "The Peanut Vendor," with a delightful sweetness. And when McKay mentions the magic of Josephine Baker, your reporter must inform you that he knows *exactly* what McKay means, from having held tightly to Miss Baker's hand for the longest moment you can imagine.

Then, it is mainly because of Buster's association with the late Policy Queen that he is in such demand as a manipulator of his own people. Jerry Batty, a businessman, offers Buster a "position" which is refused. Though broke, Buster is respected by such big shots as Spareribs Duke, the Harlem politician Homer Lake, the beautician Gypsy Nilequeen, the Colonel, who runs Neufields (a bar), and by Robert Byrd, the Glory Savior himself, for whom Buster becomes a special right hand man whose primary job is to drive the glowing white Virgin, Queen Mother, where she wants to be driven. Buster is given a new name by the lofty black Glory Savior. Henceforth he shall be known as Glory Pilgrim Progress. It is while Buster is attempting to romance a young college girl, Oleander Powers (also a Glory Savior follower known variously as Chrystal Water, and Glory Chastity), that he discovers that Mother has romantic designs on him.

Buster wastes no time in taking her up on her subtle offer. Before long they are deep into an affair, and Glory Savior is too busy running his spiritual empire to notice. But Oleander is alert and suspicious.

Meanwhile, Omar, the revolutionary, steps in and denounces Glory Savior as an agent of the evil white man whose aim is to get black people to destroy themselves. How? By abstaining from sex. Opal, a former member of Garvey's Universal-Negro-Back-to-Africa movement, turns up as Commander of Omar's yeoman. Omar preaches self help and pickets white-owned and operated Harlem businesses demanding jobs for colored. Whiffs of Pan-Africanism are aired. We see the plight of socialism, nationalism, and communism right alongside the spiritual and political exploitation in Harlem. But more distressing than these ripoffs is how closely the picture of Harlem in the 1920s correlates to Harlem today.

Finally, Madame Marie Audace and Lotta Sander return to the United States, bringing news that Aschine Palma has succeeded in taking Prince Fanti from his white bride. Aschine, a plain Afro-american girl, is now a Princess with a kingdom in West Africa.

The book ends with Buster proposing to Oleander. Marriage would make them Glory Prince and Glory Princess!

My Green Hills of Jamaica is the weakest of the three books. It is an autobiographical sketch of McKay's childhood and early adulthood years in Jamaica. The writing is poor in quality. Written near the end of McKay's life, it was obviously more unfinished than *Romance* or *Glory.*

Cedric Dover, an Anglo-Indian, author of *Half Cast* (1937) and *Know This of Race* (1943), asked McKay to do *Green Hills,* as part of a projected book Dover had in mind, to be called *East Indian, West Indian*. Dover himself would supply the other portion, about his own East Indian childhood. Aside from the fact that Dover and McKay did not share literary, social, or political views, the project never got off the ground.

In *Green Hills* McKay explains how he grew up believing that higher culture came first from England, then the rest of Europe, and finally from the United States. (It is also interesting to remember that once McKay left Jamaica, he never returned.)

Claude McKay was a young man of great personal aloofness. His mother appears to have been a woman who expressed great sympathy for people who had experienced misfortune. Many of the stories in *Gingertown* (1932), all of McKay's novels, and many of his essays, and some of his poems deal sympathetically with victims.

McKay grew up singing American Negro spirituals and fully accepting the terms of Jamaica's rigid class and caste system. Yet there is one place in *Green Hills* where the author, self-consciously and proudly, describes how a black judge effectively handles a court case.

Like other little black Britons, McKay played cricket and softball. But the African side of his heritage was present too. He made moonshine dolls. He refers to his father as a real black Scotchman.

The thin manuscript deals mainly with McKay's relation to an elderly eccentric Englishman who encourages McKay to write. The Englishman has an interest in Negro dialect and encourages McKay to use the creole which he speaks in unguarded moments. McKay would rather use the King's English, but reluctantly follows the advice of his patron. The Englishman finances the publication of McKay's first book, *Constab Ballads* (London: Watts, 1912). I took a look at a first edition recently. The format was handsome but the poems were terrible! It consists of poems McKay wrote while a young constable in Jamaica. McKay did not like the constabulary service. When he left, he spent more time in Spanish Town with his English patron.

Green Hills does not compare well to McKay's superb autobiography, *A Long Way from Home* (1937), but as a statement on the plastic years of an important international novelist, it is a valuable document.

WHITE CHARACTERS

Willard Motley, along with a minority of other black American authors, from the beginnings of American literature to the present, wrote fiction in which the question of race was not a central theme.

Most of Motley's characters were white. There is a black American tradition of fiction by black authors dealing solely with white characters. Examples are Zora Neal Hurston's *Seraph on the Suwanne*, Richard Wright's *Savage Holiday*, James Baldwin's *Giovanni's Room*, Ann Petry's *Country Place*, Samuel R. Delany's *Dhalgren*, and Charles Perry's *Portrait of a Young Man Drowning*.

Many black writers, on the other hand, have made fiction about black characters but with no overwhelming special commitment to racial problems. Examples among them are Charles Wright, Ishmael Reed, Jean Toomer, William Demby, John Wideman, LeRoi Jones (Amiri Baraka), and Robert Boles.

There is also a long tradition of white writers writing about black people. One of the most successful is Gertrude Stein's "Melanctha," in *Three Lives*. Gertrude Stein's Melanctha emerges as a "real person." Most white writers, however, have invented black characters who represent "problems" of society, or who are idiots or savages. Exceptions in varying degrees would be Herman Melville's *Benito Cereno*, William Faulkner's *Light in August*, Harriet Beecher Stowe's *Uncle Tom's Cabin*, Carl Van Vechten's *Nigger Heaven*, William Styron's *The Confessions of Nat Turner*, Bernard Malamud's novel *The Tenants* and his story "Angel Levine," and Shane Steven's *Way Up Town in Another World*. These authors, in these books, are concerned with race as well as with other aspects of the question of identity.

Williard Motley always saw his characters as real people, never solely as sociological puzzles or ethnic beings. Motley's Italians have social habits that are characteristic of the Chicago Italian American community, but the reader is also allowed to see and feel them, to know them on other levels.

When Robert Bone, in *The Negro Novel in America,* accuses Motley of nearly plagiarizing Richard Wright's *Native Son,* Bone must not have thought much further than what the book reviewers of the day were saying. Fact is, *Knock on Any Door,* the Motley book Bone refers to came along in a tradition well-worn. Motley simply wrote a type of novel that had been popular since Stendhal's *The Red and the Black. Native Son* was hardly the best example of a prototype for *Knock on Any Door.* Motley was certainly no innovator. But neither were Theodore Dreiser or Sinclair Lewis. Whose shoulders were they standing on? The answer is too obvious.

Generally, Williard Motley did not and has not received serious critical attention until recently, in such periodicals as *Proof: The Yearbook of American Bibliographical and Textual Studies, The Negro American Literature Forum,* and *Resources for American Literary Study.* The serious Motley scholars are Jerome Klinkowitz, who uncovered Motley's literary archives, Jill Weyant, Ann Rayson, Charles and Karen Wood, Bob Fleming, James Giles, and John O'Brien. A few popular literary studies of Motley in relation to modern and contemporary Negro fiction have appeared, but they have, almost without exception, dealt with everything written by blacks as though the racial reference constituted a fixed form, a genre.

Like many other writers of both quality and commercial fiction, Motley left, after his death, many unpublished manuscripts. Constance Webb and Michel Fabre indicate that Richard Wright left a long, detailed diary, at least one unpublished novel, and many shorter works. There is an unpublished autobiography of Jean Toomer. Claude McKay left several unpublished novels and a number of miscellaneous manuscripts. Well-known is the fact that Ernest Hemingway left unfinished *Islands in the Stream* and several other manuscripts. John Berryman's *Recovery* was not finished. The natural question that arises is: If the work is inferior or unfinished, should it be published? I can say without reservations that the publication of Willard Motley's diaries will not damage his reputation. The quality of thinking and feeling expressed in them, even the writing, can only enhance his image. They are, so far, his best published works.

It is not unusual for an author's unpublished manuscripts to reveal a side of the person not previously known. Richard Wright's "Island of Hallucination," Claude McKay's "Romance in Marseilles" and "Harlem Glory," and Jean Toomer's unpublished fiction and autobiography serve respectively as indices to the fact that these writers have been dealt with in critical terms based solely on the range of their published works, which, obviously, do not tell the full story. Willard Motley's unpublished works reveal a writer who tried many techniques and themes, sometimes with real success, as with the book *Adventure,* a sensitive account of bumming across the country in the spirit of Jack London and before Jack Kerouac's *On the Road* appeared.

Motley's *Adventure* indicates a whole new aspect of a writer the public has not been aware of. In an essay on Motley by Charles Wood, Karen Wood is quoted. She says Motley's "view of Los Angeles and its citizens shows such an affirmative love for humanity that one can never again view Motley simply as a traditional naturalist . . ." ("The *Adventure* Manuscript: New Light on Willard Motley's Naturalism," *Negro American Literature Forum*) Charles Wood's point is that Motley was not limited to "a sordid and deterministic view of man."

William Motley was a conventional writer and a conservative person. In an essay by Jerome Klinkowitz and James R. Giles called "The Emergence of Willard Motley in Black American Literature," (NALF), the reader witnesses an exchange of letters between Motley, Chester Himes, and Carl Van Vechten—subject: Himes's controversial novel, *Lonely Crusade,* which deals with a young Negro struggling to maintain his own sense of integrity while being used by American communist and labor groups. Motley apparently assumed Himes's book represented an attack on whites. Motley wrote and published a negative review of the book, then wrote Himes an apology for his inability to like the book.

Carl Van Vechten, meanwhile, saw something tragic and something sympathetic in Motley. Motley was no doubt a tragic figure. He was also certainly a very sympathetic person. But he was also sensitively intelligent and a totally committed writer. Writing was almost his whole life.

The extent of Motley's sincerity is dramatically demonstrated in the diaries. He was a thoughtful and shy person; even during the single time I talked to him, one day in the summer of 1960 in Chicago, this was obvious. These diaries reflect a passionate young man with an optimistic outlook. Motley was more interested in expression and impression than in meaning and reason. His published novels, the manuscript *Adventure,* and the diaries support this judgment. He had a democratic spirit. It is given expression throughout the diaries in Englewood High School episodes and later in the traveling episodes. When Motley was abused, he did not strike back; he tried to find in himself the strength to withstand the abuse. He was instinctively nonviolent—hence the irony of the "tough little iron man" and the "tough" looking expressions on his face in photographs that appeared on the covers and jackets of his novels. Fighting back, as the diaries indicate, was an activity Motley managed in a more subtle manner. His sense of himself was hardly racial, though he never denied his racial heritage. Most important to Willard Motley's vision of "unadorned" life was his lower middle-class outlook.

Motley was devoted to beauty and especially to the idea of male beauty. Nick Romano, hero of *Knock on Any Door,* was based in part on a handsome Mexican named Tino N—, whom Motley met while traveling through Denver, where N— served time in a detention home. For a writer as realistically, as graphically, as naturalistically oriented as Willard Motley, the whole idea of internalizing certain aspects of real persons for the purposes of fiction was a natural process. In trying to help Tino, Motley assumes the role he later assigns to one of his characters, a writer, Grant Holloway. Holloway is white.

In the diaries Motley invents a reality based on his own life. When he describes the process of inventing and living with his characters, especially with Nick, it is with the same compassion and care he gives to real people in real life, before, during, and after the writing of *Knock on Any Door.*

There is an innocent sort of intelligence in the diaries. Motley relates his many conversations with friends and he finds, almost always, a lot of joy in the "deep" discoveries about "life" during these talks.

While in high school he refers to his existence as an "ugly desert."

He sees himself as very plain. He finds himself seeking handsome friends, seeking "the beautiful in life." Even this early he describes schoolmates who resemble Nick.

This, a condensed version of the diaries, begins January 1, 1926, and ends June 1, 1943, when Willard Motley was thirty-three, four years before the publication of *Knock on Any Door,* his most celebrated previously published work.

DON, HERE IS MY PEPPERMINT STRIPED SHIRT

There were a lot things I didn't understand till I moved to New York. I moved there from the midwest in 1966. Once I knew certain cultural pockets in the city, I had a frame of reference for understanding, for example, the emotional restraint and the sophistication of Donald Barthelme's fictional world.

Don and I did not meet till the year my second novel, *No,* was published (1973). Faith and Kirk Sale gave a Christmas party that year. They lived downstairs in the same building Don lived at 113 West Eleventh Street, across the street from Grace Paley (one of his closest friends). Faith was involved with the magazine *Fiction* and had just accepted one of my stories. She invited me and the woman I was living with over for the festivities. It wasn't a big crowd, a few people from publishing.

Donald Barthelme was there. He looked like a Mormon in aviator glasses, denim workshirt, and jeans. He was friendly in a subdued way. He was drinking scotch. We talked quietly in a corner for a while, mostly about how much he disliked going up to Buffalo in the cold to teach creative writing.

We also talked about the elegant old prints he was using to illustrate his stories. The prints were in the public domain, he said. He took what he wanted from old medical books and the like. These pictures fascinated me as much as his prose.

I remember thinking, He doesn't look like a man who is about to commit suicide. (A year or two before, somebody had written an article about Barthelme that appeared in the *New York Times Magazine.*

Near the end the journalist said that he wouldn't be surprised if Donald Barthelme eventually committed suicide. Well, that journalist's tentative credentials as a reader of the future are permanently shot.)

It was a quiet party. Not much moving around. There was, though, one animated but obnoxious young woman, from publishing, who managed to get Don to take her upstairs to his place so that he could show her something or other—maybe an etching. When they came back half an hour later all the animation had left her face.

Occasionally I ran into Don on the street in the Village. One Monday I saw him near Sixth Avenue. The day before, I had read in the Sunday *Times* a letter he'd written on the matter of a certain young man who had been writing Donald Barthelme stories and publishing them under the name Donald Bartheleme.

"Are you going to sue?" This was the beginning of the period when everybody was suing everybody for the slightest offense.

"No," Don said. "I asked him to stop. He said he would. That's good enough for me."

In the summer of 1977, Gotham Book Mart in New York held a book signing for William Burroughs. Penguin had just reissued his 1953 novel, *Junky,* in paperback. Burroughs was upstairs signing copies of the book. The place was crowded as hell and it was hot. People were spilling out onto the sidewalk. We were drinking wine from plastic cups.

I went outside and joined a small group of people sitting on the steps leading down into the store. Don was sitting there with another man. He introduced the gentleman as W. S. Merwin. Although I knew Merwin's work and liked it, he and I didn't have much to say to each other.

What I do remember of that occasion is a conversation Don and I had about the shirt I was wearing.

"That's a very cool-looking shirt, Clarence."

"Thanks. I like it too."

"I wish it were mine. I like the peppermint stripes."

"I'll leave it to you in my will."

Don smiled. He said something else but I don't remember precisely what. It was probably clever. (By the way, in the jacket photograph of his 1986 novel, *Paradise,* Don is wearing a shirt just like mine.)

The next time I ran into Don was in Fort Collins, Colorado, in the winter of 1978. He was there to give a reading at Colorado State University. At the time I was living in Boulder, Colorado, about an hour away. In the freezing cold, I drove over for the reading and the reception.

He read slowly and carefully, keeping his voice at an even pitch. You had to really listen to the words. The Barthelme humor was there but easy to miss because his voice didn't warn you. He was the straight man delivering the lines of the other Barthelme, the comic.

At the reception we talked about critics, especially the ones who had recently been working on so-called postmodern fiction. Some of those critics had recently written about his work and mine too. Don didn't care much for what they had to say about him although what they said was very positive.

After the formal reception a few students—Yusef Komunyakaa among them, I think—gave a reception for Don in a nearby house where some of them lived. The students knew Barthelme's work: they had plenty of good scotch on hand.

Most of the action was in the kitchen. Don, however, sat quietly on the couch in the living room. He never moved all evening. Once in a while a student would muster up enough courage to go and sit beside him and talk a bit. But it was clear that such conversations were hard to sustain because Don's responses were cryptic. They did keep his glass filled, though.

In the early part of the evening, I hung out mostly in the kitchen where the food was. Later, the host played some very special blues records. At this point I withdrew to a corner. I sipped white wine and listened till eleven-thirty. I dreaded night driving and there was no heat in my car. I shook Don's hand and said good-bye. I said good night to the host. That was the last time I saw Donald Barthelme.

In the fall of 1989, when my wife told me about his death, I felt a sadness for the loss of something that had never been. It is the same sadness I feel when I look at the yellowed pages of a book that has been in my life, unread, for more than twenty years.

IN SEARCH OF REBECCA

The hard questions usually have no simple answers. For me, writing stories is the best means of dealing with difficult questions of ethics, morality, and philosophy. In confronting perplexing questions in my fiction and poetry, I've achieved an odd kind of success. Often I have no idea how to formulate the question, let alone the answer, before I struggle with it through the process of writing. The writing then becomes the avenue into the complex nature of the question itself. If I come out of the process with a clearer sense of the question, and with no answer—which is more often the case than not—I am satisfied. That's the odd success, I mean. I stopped, for example, asking, "Who made me?" "Where'd I come from?" when I was twelve. I stopped asking, "Is there a God?" by age twenty-one, after which everything, in Gide's words, seemed "downhill."

Finding life's questions is the business of fiction and poetry. But it's impossible to separate the writing from the living and its stories. They are two narrow highways running parallel through an unclear and unpredictable landscape. I write to understand my life, and to understand the lives of people who interest me. My family, for example, interests me. I want to understand what the stories of their lives meant and mean. And we know that great stories can be parables for our own lives. They serve to show us how long we have been at our best, how the patterns of human behavior don't change all that much, and also how long we've been at our worst. Stories lay out for us possibilities for the future.

While recently rereading Genesis, I dwelled for some time on the brief story of Rebecca. I am aware that a small number of African Americans have traditionally claimed ancestry in ancient

Israel, tracing their lineage back to one of the twelve tribes. I am also aware of the symbolic importance of Jewish biblical stories to the religious feelings of African slaves in the colonies, and the spirituals they forged from the hardship of their lives. But these two facts didn't concern me when I reread the story of Rebecca.

Her story conjured up for me a seedbed of questions about human behavior that I'd been dealing with both in life and in my fiction. Questions regarding the negative aspects of life, such as selfishness, deceit, pettiness, shrewdness, cruelty, evil, complicity in evildoing, materialism, treachery, naturally interest a writer of fiction. So do questions about the positive, such as obedience, goodness, generosity, kindness, honor, trust, suffering, tactfulness, ambition, devout faith, piousness, scrupulousness, the sense of nobility. Rebecca's life calls to mind each of these traits and tendencies. Her story is a story within stories.

Who, then, is Rebecca? Fixed firmly in the mother-line of the family of Abraham, Rebecca is the daughter of Bethuel and Milcah, sister of Laban, wife of Isaac, mother of Esau and Jacob. She is mentioned only in a few brief episodes of Genesis, and only her burial in Abraham's cave, not even her death, is recorded. But Rebecca's generosity and kindness are demonstrated in the first episode in which she appears. Abraham's servant, Eliezer, on a trip from Canaan to find a wife for Abraham's youngest son, forty-year-old Isaac, meets her at the Padan Aram (Aram-Nahariam / northern Mesopotamia) community well where the family's water is drawn. Though she's wooed with jewelry, it is probably not the glitter of gold that ultimately wins her over. Rebecca's selfless generosity in this scene, where she insists on watering all the camels of Eliezer's caravan, sets the stage for her marriage to Isaac.

Rebecca marries Isaac in his mother's tent (by going to bed with him) and becomes a devoted wife. Later, while the couple is on a trip to Gerar, when Isaac tells the Philistines that Rebecca is his sister to protect her from being seized by them, Rebecca effectively plays the part of sister. She and Isaac both obviously believe in the use of deception in an emergency. Twenty years later she gives birth to twin sons, Esau and Jacob, destined from birth to be in conflict with each other. Esau is a hunter. He's physical. Jacob is spiritual. He's quiet.

Years pass and their father Isaac grows old and blind. One day

Rebecca, probably eavesdropping, overhears her husband telling his eldest son, Esau, that it is time for an important ritual. But first, Esau must bring his father venison. Isaac plans, after the ritual of eating the venison, to bestow, according to Jewish law, the patriarchal blessing of heirship upon his eldest son. Directing the family bloodline was of the utmost importance.

But there seem to be some problems with Esau. Rebecca and her husband believe Esau to be unqualified for a quiet spiritual life of devotion to God and family, the most desirable qualities in a son entrusted to carry on the family birthright. Both parents disapprove of Esau's marriage to a Hittite woman of Canaan. Overhearing the conversation between Isaac and Esau, Rebecca hurries to her youngest and favorite son, Jacob. She convinces him that he must intercede. By pretending to be Esau, she tells Jacob that he can trick his blind father, and receive the irrevocable blessing, becoming heir. She cooks goat meat and gives it to Jacob. He, taking it in to his father, apparently convinces Isaac that he is Esau, and receives the blessing.

If Rebecca gambles, she loses, because Jacob has to go away to his mother's birthplace to avoid the wrath of his brother, Esau. And Jacob is gone for twenty years, during which time his life is miserable. Rebecca's scheme to get the heirship for her favorite son ends, ironically, in her loss of his presence for twenty years. But Jacob does marry a woman, Rachel, in the desired family line. It's a bitter victory. And, finally, as the patriarch of his own tribe, Jacob is destined to become the everlasting symbol of the birth of Israel.

Despite the strong symbolism of their stories and the archetypal natures of Rebecca, her husband Isaac, and her twin sons Esau and Jacob, the few brief episodes containing Rebecca herself spoke to me on a profoundly personal level. In some very essential ways, Rebecca reminded me of the hardworking, generous, strong, quietly ambitious, and determined, though relatively powerless, women in my own family, going all the way back to my great-grandmother, Rebecca, on my father's side.

Every time I teach Jean Toomer's story "Becky," I think about this white great-grandmother about whom so little is known. Toomer's story starts, "Becky was the white woman who had two Negro sons. She's dead . . ." The story takes place in the backwoods of Georgia in, say, the 1880s or 1890s. In the end Becky's house (built by the black and the white townsfolk) falls in on her, becoming her tomb. In other words, her neighbors' condescension and grudging generosity eventually help to kill her.

My great-grandmother Rebecca Lankford (a.ka. Rebecca Talbot, who was white) gave birth to my grandmother, Anna Bowling, in 1878 in Oglethorpe County. She brought bastardy charges against William T. Bowling, a young white man, which probably served to save my great-grandfather, Stephen Bowling, a black man (born 1861), from death by lynching. Stephen and William no doubt grew up together on the Bowling plantation.

Rebecca was poor and, like the rest of her immediate family, largely uneducated. I can only imagine the pain she endured and the possible deceit she had to exercise to survive a racist social system that doubly condemned her for having a child out of wedlock and for breaking the racial code.

On the black side of my family it is well-known that Rebecca lied to the community to save Stephen's life—she even threatened suicide if any harm came to him. The court records of course do not show any of this, only the bastardy charges against a young white man. Rebecca's life is an ironic metaphor for and commentary on the racialized system based on whiteness as privilege that has dogged America since the end of the Colonial period.

Rebecca gave up Anna soon after birth. Anna was cared for by a black woman, Edith Jackson, till her grandmother (my great-great-grandmother) Harriet Bowling (born a slave in 1833 on Thornberry Bowling's plantation) took charge of her at about age six, adopting her legally a few years later.

Like Rebecca of Genesis, my grandmother too probably had to find subversive ways to survive in a world that provided no place for her. After all, she was, in appearance, a white woman (and remained *legally* white) who was culturally black.

In a sense, such lives—Becky's, my great-grandmother Rebecca's, and my grandmother Anna's—are stories about powerlessness. When a powerless person commits an act of wrongdoing, moral and ethical issues swirl around the person like buzzards around a carcass, just as they do around the powerful. But the implications and ramifications are different.

The main point I'm trying to make here is this: Like the biblical Rebecca, a relatively powerless woman, women like Toomer's Becky, and women of my great-grandmothers' and grandmothers' generations, in order to give expression to their legitimate personal, domestic, social, or political concerns, often were compelled to behave in ways that can be characterized as deceitful, mean-spirited, unscrupulous, or cruel. This is almost certainly the case with the biblical Rebecca, who was up against the power of the patriarchal family and community.

I think understanding such communities, and their histories of particulars, gives a writer the basis for understanding how powerlessness works. In the communities I grew up in, both in the North and South, I remember parents (but especially mothers) worrying about who their offspring married. I remember a neighbor woman, a friend of my mother's, going to great extremes, but in a covert manner, to try to sabotage her son's affair with a particular girl of whom she (the mother) didn't approve.

Whether or not we have power we can use openly, and because we want things to go our way, we sometimes try to influence the future turn of events through taking certain actions. With her act of deception, Rebecca tries to assert her influence on the future of her family.

But does Rebecca think about the consequences of her action? As a child, I was told to think before acting. Either Rebecca doesn't think about the consequences of her deception, or she weighs the possible outcome against doing nothing, and decides to go ahead with her plan because the possible problems stemming from the deception seem to her far less than the problem of Jacob *not* receiving the blessing. Or, she doesn't care.

Rebecca loves both of her sons, but Jacob is her favorite. In her own judgment, no doubt, she is acting as a good mother when she devises a scheme—derived from her inability to act openly—to give Jacob an advantage over his brother. We all know, as painful as it sometimes is to admit, that parents have favorites.

The difficult question remains: Is it okay to commit an act of wrongdoing in the interest of a perceived good? Rebecca tricked Isaac. In a short story I wrote called "Ten Pecan Pies," a wife (based on my grandmother Ada) tricks her selfish husband into turning over his prized pecans so that she can bake pecan pies as Christmas gifts for the community. Her deception, like Rebecca's, one might argue, was ultimately for a good cause.

But does that *justify* the act? That is one of the difficult questions. Yet, before we get to such a hard reckoning, we have to ask: Is Rebecca merely carrying out the wish of her husband? In other words, is she, by taking upon herself the burden of the "evil" act, letting Isaac off the hook? In this paradigm, Rebecca knows her husband so well, and is so obedient, that she saves him the difficulty of rejecting his oldest son—the rightful inheritor—in favor of his youngest, who is clearly her (and secretly his) choice for the position.

If Rebecca's deception is ultimately the act of a loyal but powerless wife carrying out the will of her husband, then she is rehabilitated, at least in literary terms, from her role as a villain. On the other hand, a deterministic reading would leave one believing that everything that happened was preordained. Such a reading would also exonerate Rebecca and Jacob of all wrongdoing. Among my grandmothers and their church friends, there was a common expression: "Well, honey, it's the will of God." In other words, they felt powerless to change the situation in question. That always puzzled me. I couldn't understand how they knew what God was thinking.

Powerless people act in ways that are not always easy to understand. When I was growing up, I couldn't count the times I saw the women of my own family take responsibilities or burdens upon themselves to protect their menfolk from having to deal with some unpleasantness. They not only accepted their place or role in both home and church, but went out of their way to make life easier for the men. This may have been noble and selfless, but it was not necessarily right. Actually, I think it was, ultimately, not good for the women or the men.

But these were strong women. Rebecca, like Isaac's mother Sarah, was a strong home person. Rebecca was the manifestation of Isaac's home. Her sons were who they were culturally because of her pervasive presence in the home as its defining agent. In this sense, she reminds me of women in my own family—my mother, my grandmothers, who helped define for me my culture. I tried to pay tribute to such women in my novel *Such was the Season,* which is about a week in the life of an elderly black woman in Atlanta.

I feel an empathy with such women, which is sometimes noted in reviews of my fiction and poetry. This identification with the female perhaps stems from that part of myself that is itself female, as well as perhaps from my close contact with a house full of women while growing up. For example, it took courage and tenacity for women like my grandmother Anna to endure. Perhaps I instinctively understood who she was in the face of what she had to do to get through her life.

In the end, do we know who Rebecca is? Rebecca as a virgin girl by the well, who volunteers to water a caravan of ten camels, is the same Rebecca who, many years later, urges her son Jacob to deceive his father. We know that her life has many implications. One is the notion that even from a base of powerlessness, a person can sometimes exert a degree of influence. But, as with any human life, the task is to see the whole life before passing judgment. How do those one or two moments of deception, of breaking the rules, fit into a whole life of hospitality, trust, compassion, faith, and generosity?

Ultimately, and when viewed in retrospect, breaking the rules or even breaking the law is not always bad. The serfs of Russia broke the law when they rose up against the ruling class. Rosa Parks broke the law when she refused to move to the back of the bus. Rebecca of Genesis is a good person who breaks the rules. The result is biblical history.

AN APPOINTMENT WITH JOHN O'HARA

Though I can't see in my own work any influence from John O'Hara, I grew up reading his novels and short stories. Hardly children's literature, right? Apparently they interested me and I often enjoyed them a great deal. And probably in some remote way, learned something about writing from reading them.

When O'Hara died in 1970 I still had not developed much conscious interest in fiction of manners but have since (in a sense) gone in that direction—I'm interested in writing about whole towns, whole cities. (See *Emergency Exit, 1979*). Also the fact that O'Hara's biggest cultural contribution seems to have been as a conscious social historian, rather than as the controlled stylist he's often called, is important to me because the social approach is the main tradition black writers have supported and imitated. I am not in that tradition as a writer, but I care about it, study it, know it as a critic, a scholar, and as an African American. It has meaning for me. If the tough guy writers of the twenties and thirties influenced anybody they certainly influenced black writers like Chester Himes and Willard Motley. Even Charles Wright has never pretended to like the sharp, lean style of Hemingway. And in terms of style O'Hara is not worlds apart from Hemingway, though I know this is not a popular thing to say to an O'Hara fan.

O'Hara wrote about characters of my parents' generation, and though they were white, the mores, the social habits, the aspirations of his characters were not strange or remote to me, not all that different from those I witnessed in people around me, who were mostly colored, African American, black, and Black with a capital B. This may be to O'Hara's credit: that he got beneath the social surfaces, in some way, to the human level, as it expresses itself socially.

His people were social animals who did not recognize this fact about themselves. He ripped the façade away without being didactic. That is a literary achievement. It did not matter to me that my social habits didn't match those of the characters in *Appointment in Samarra,* or that I didn't care about labor movements or political organizations. I was amazed by O'Hara's god-like control of his characters who never understood that they were tragic.

For me his work is the documented proof that hard work, clean sex, and going to church on Sunday won't make anybody happy ever after.

WALLACE THURMAN
AND THE NIGGERATTI MANOR

Perhaps best known for his successful 1929 Broadway play *Harlem* (written in collaboration with William Jourdan Rapp), Wallace Thurman is all but forgotten today. There is some documented evidence that Thurman wrote a number of other plays, none of which were ever produced. He was born in Salt Lake City in 1902, and he died in New York City in 1934, young and destitute. Author of three novels, *The Blacker the Berry: A Novel of Negro Life* (1929), *Infants of the Spring* (1932), and *The Interne* (1932), the latter written in collaboration with Abraham L. Furman, Thurman also published thirteen articles (on subjects as diverse as Christmas, Brigham Young, and Harlem). While working in Hollywood, he wrote the screenplays for two motion pictures—one about resistance to forced sterilization and poverty, and not about race in any way. He published four short stories, one in his own magazine, *Fire!!* (1926).

In the editorial comment for the first and only issue of *Fire!!*, Thurman proclaimed a philosophy of aesthetic freedom for young black writers as forceful as Ezra Pound's and Wyndham Lewis's *Blast 1* did for the expatriates. All the youthful "vortex" of what Pound called "sun, energy, sombre emotion, clean-drawing, disgust, penetrating analysis," permeates the pages of *Fire!! Blast,* too, made only one appearance.

Thurman's blast against "sociological problems and propaganda" in literature, in the form of his magazine, was new on the Afro-American literary scene. The issue carried works by Gwendolyn Brooks, Zora Neale Hurston, Langston Hughes, and the artist Aaron

Douglas. *Fire!!* came eleven years after *Blast* and its announcement of Vorticism ("We stand for the Reality of the Present—"), and three years before Eugene Jolas's *Transition,* with its manifesto for "The Revolution of the Word." All three efforts aimed in the same direction, stated well by the *Transition* manifesto: "The imagination in search of a fabulous world is autonomous and unconfined."

I have chosen to focus on Thurman's *Infants of the Spring* (New York: Furman, 1932) because I think it is worthy of far more attention that it has ever received. It certainly deserves a chance with present and future readers. I feel this way because the book probes—without giving any answers—important issues of race and art.

Infants of the Spring is set in Harlem, in a rooming house nicknamed Niggeratti Manor, and as such it attempts to satirize what Thurman saw as the failure of the Harlem Renaissance. The main characters are Raymond Taylor, a troubled and confused writer; his white roommate, Stephen Jorgenson, who seems to be hanging out in Harlem in order to have an exotic experience; Euphoria Blake, the landlady; Lucille, Raymond's best female friend; Aline and Janet, two young women into free love and booze and whatever else is available; Paul Arbian, a cynical and witty painter; Eustance, an opera singer filled with disdain for his own Afro-American heritage; Samuel Carter, a white man who thinks of himself as a liberal and tries his best to help the members of the artistic colony; Barbara Nitsky (The Countess), a young white woman from Greenwich Village now living in Harlem, where the living seems, for her, a lot easier; and a staggering array of minor characters, most of whom seem to be based on real, identifiable people, contemporaries of Wallace Thurman.

Raymond Taylor seems to be a persona for the author. He certainly speaks out (almost always in contradictory terms) on issues of art, race, and sex in ways one can easily associate with Wallace Thurman's own thinking on these topics. Raymond, like Thurman himself, was suspicious of the racial artistic rebirth called the Harlem Renaissance. He doubted its authenticity because he felt that it had been created by journalistic hype—"the foundation of the building [Niggertti Manor] was composed of crumbling stone." (Whether or not this is true, it is certainly true that many movements, before and since, have been founded on questionable foundations. Two examples: The Lost Generation and the Beat Generation were journalistic inventions, yet some participants in each produced works of outstanding quality.)

As I have already suggested, in the matter of the editorial policy of *Fire!!,* Thurman took the position that Negro artists and writers of his day should be free to do what they chose (to paraphrase Langston Hughes) and not worry about how anybody might react. Well, Raymond takes that position too, denouncing any obligation for social responsibility. Yet Raymond speaks out in favor of racial pride and Afro-American cultural heritage, and keeping them ever present in the art. Surely, some degree of social responsibility is expressed when the cultural heritage finds its way into a work of art no matter how free that work might be from propagandistic aims. Raymond wants it both ways, and there is nothing wrong with that. His fight is for absolute artistic freedom.

Raymond is as passionate about art as a character in a novel can possibly be. He longs to "transcend and survive the transitional age in which he was living: but he doubts that he has the genius to create a literary work of lasting quality." He no doubt echoes Thurman himself.

But it is Raymond's contradictory stand that makes him all the more human and interesting. He attacks Samuel Carter as a "phony Left Wing radical." Raymond insists that Samuel is, at heart, a Right Wing conservative who only pretends to have the interests of the Negro at heart. Yet he defends the Countess Barbara's right to live the sporting life, as a prized white woman, among black men. At the same time, he looks with disdain upon Janet for her attraction to Stephen ("Jesus, are you Negro women as bad as Negro men?").

When Eustance refuses to accept a job Samuel has found for him singing spirituals, Raymond is careful not to take sides. He defends Eustance's right to sing only opera and at the same time detests Eustance's refusal to embrace his own heritage by singing spirituals. Eventually Raymond tries to bring Eustance around to accepting the job.

Yet it is Raymond's relationship with Stephen that is most contradictory, complex, and subtle. On the one hand, he seems to have set himself as Stephen's instructor on Negro life, as a sort of tour guide of Harlem and the manor. Raymond wants Stephen to see the universal aspects of life in Harlem and at the same time to appreciate those cultural factors that are unique to the community. The two men are the opposite of each other, on a surface level, and mirror images underneath. In Conrad's terms, they are soulmates. Stephen, in one sense, is slumming, and in another, he could not be more innocently serious about his interest in the people of the manor and beyond, in the neighborhood. For him they are culturally exotic, yet not in the least exotic because he *does* recognize that universal element Raymond wants him to see.

Raymond and Stephen sleep together. Although a specific homosexual relationship is never spelled out, the emotional quality of intimacy seems to be there. Thurman had already demonstrated in his first novel an interest in male homosexuality with his character Alva. Here, in *Infants of the Spring,* Raymond seems jealous and protective of Stephen while he is carrying on with Aline. Predictably, Raymond refuses to admit his jealousy and dismisses the affair as silly.

Halfway through the book, there is an important scene where Raymond is walking moodily through Central Park. Thurman would have us believe that this is the ultimate moment of Raymond's potential, and perhaps it is. Raymond dreams of breaking "the chains which held him to the racial rack. He wants to carry a blazing beacon to the top of Mount Olympus." In other words, Raymond hopes he is a genius and not simply another talented Negro with "no standards, no elasticity, no pregnant germ plasm." The narrator tells us that Raymond's mind, during this walk, is "chaotic and deranged." The tone assumed by the narrator here is a bit unexpected and not entirely convincing. Yet, at least for the moment, the condition of Raymond's mind, that is, a mind of "attractive brilliance" without maturity, saves Raymond from stupidity. And Thurman elsewhere in the book reinforces what we can expect from Raymond by quoting Maxim Gorky: "A man slightly possessed is not only more agreeable to me; he is altogether more plausible . . ." So, we are expected to ride with Raymond's confusion, his contradictions, his "adolescent brain," and at least celebrate his potential, because, again, like Gorky's ideal, this man is "not quite achieved . . . not yet very wise, a little mad, possessed."

Raymond, nevertheless, knows a few things about himself. He knows his own potential for self-destruction, his own tendency to corrupt rather than cultivate his difference. And this, I think, gets at exactly what Thurman wants us to see most about Raymond's personality: "There had been no catharsis, no intellectual metabolism." And in this moment of growthlessness, "race consciousness" is Raymond's largest trap. The fact that he sees it as a trap does not mean that he is ashamed of his heritage. On the contrary, Raymond would have the boundaries of his own cultural frame of reference enlarged and he would carry it with him to the mountaintop. He does not wish to leave himself and his history behind, but to change our perception of both. But he fails to realize that in American society his dream of freedom from "race consciousness" has no context in which it can be understood without contradiction. (This is a familiar theme in nineteenth-century American immigrant popular fiction. Bernardino Ciambelli comes to mind.) So, little wonder his walk ends in "Futile introspection, desperate flagellations . . . in darkness and despair."

Raymond's relations with the other characters also reveal his unresolved many-sidedness. With his landlady, Euphoria (who has been a feminist and a Greenwich Village Left Wing radical), he is strangely tolerant of human shortcomings, having no caustic responses to her many silly positions on art and life. Raymond sees in Paul Arbian a true artist and a sincere spirit. (In the end, Paul commits suicide, doomed, as the manor he named is also doomed.) Lucille is the one who meets Raymond at places beyond the manor. She clearly wants to keep her distance. Her posture seems to say that she likes Raymond but dislikes his life, such as it is. After all, he is a writer who cannot write. Raymond feels both pity and contempt for poor Pelham Gaylord, who eventually is jailed for raping a neighbor's daughter.

These main characters are probably based on real persons Thurman knew in Harlem. They are far more interesting and complex than the many minor characters because there is evidence that the author managed to take his creations some distance from the real models and to invest them with a sort of life of their own. On the other hand, the minor characters are flat and are mainly of historical interest because they are often recognizable as figures (stick figures?) in a roman à clef. Thurman's artist friend Bruce Nugent was the inspiration for Paul Arbian. Well-known Harlem personality Mrs. Sidney was the model for Euphoria Blake. DeWitt Clint, the West Indian poet, is probably based on Eric Walrond. Sweetie Mary Carr is probably Thurman's fictional version of Zora Neale Hurston. Dr. Parks is Dr. Alain Locke? Or is Locke the model for Thurman's Dr. Manfred Trout? I suspect that Cedric Williams is based on Cedric Dover, the anthropologist and editor of *American Negro Art.*

All of these figures and more turn up for Niggeratti Manor's first and last salon. They are paraded and made to spout their points of view, often revealing narrow-mindedness or worse, on art and race, on the New Negro, on Picasso, Matisse, Gauguin, Sargent, Renoir, Gertrude Stein, jazz, on modernism generally, you name it. (In fact, it is the soapbox forum throughout the novel that is most annoying.) Yet the dedicated trivia seeker might easily identify characters based on Aaron Douglas, novelist Rudolph Fisher, poet Countee Cullen, and others. I have little doubt that Doris Westmore, short story writer, and her cousin, poet Hazel Jamison, are based on Boston novelist Dorothy West *(The Living Is Easy* [1948]) and her cousin. In using real persons as models, Thurman attempted a difficult task. Real people and their beliefs, undigested and untransformed, never work in fiction. Dante, in his *Inferno,* succeeded because he got beyond the original motive and turned his heretics into creations no longer linked to their models.

Infants of the Spring is not a great book but it is a serious book, a passionate and painfully conceived book. The style is often as delicate as that of F. Scott Fitzgerald's, but the point of view, on the other hand, wobbles too much. Like Thurman's first novel (which is much better known), it has flaws, the flaws one expects to find in early work. Vincent van Gogh's "Potato Eaters," an early painting, is seriously flawed in a way the works done at Arles are not. Cézanne's early works are flawed. So are most first, and for that matter, second novels. Wallace Thurman died at the age of thirty-two. Most American writers have not published their first novels by that age. Works that show a writer or painter reaching (to paraphrase Rilke) all glory and all time, are rare. Wallace Thurman wanted to create such work but did not. There is no way to know if he would have managed to do so had he lived longer.

AUTHOR'S NOTE

The following three essays were commissioned in the late eighties for a book on the history of literary magazines titled *American Literary Magazines: The Twentieth Century* (Connecticut: Greenwood Press, 1992). I was especially pleased to accept the assignment because in my own career literary magazines generally were central and essential.

Once I started doing the research I felt more than the usual pleasure of detective work. Ferreting out the human stories behind the periodicals was especially interesting to me. If my reader finds even half the amount of pleasure I had in researching and writing them, I will be pleased.

LOOKING AT THE *DIAL*

In May 1880 when, in Chicago, Francis F. Browne started publishing a magazine he called the *Dial,* he was aligning himself with a spiritual and intellectual tradition. Margaret Fuller and Ralph Waldo Emerson edited the first *Dial*, a quarterly, in Boston from 1840 to 1844. They had been interested, among other things, in providing a forum for transcendentalism, broad views of theology, and philosophical investigations. Sixteen years later, in Cincinnati, Rev. Moncure D. Conway attempted to carry on the *Dial* tradition, but his magazine lasted only a year. Browne's *Dial* began as a monthly, and the first issue carried an essay on the original *Dial* by Norman C. Perkins. Browne's employer, General McClurg, published the magazine under the imprint of his house, Jansen, McClurg & Company.

Browne, a printer, had earlier bought stock in the *Western Monthly,* and in 1871 he became the magazine's editor, later changing the title to the *Lakeside Monthly*. This publication folded due to money problems in 1874, and from then until 1879 Browne was without a magazine and also in poor health. In 1880, he went to work for McClurg. Browne edited the *Dial* for the company as its house organ until 1892, when he bought it and renamed its publisher the Dial Company. He had already taken on his brother, F. C. Browne, as business manager in 1888, and now he enlisted William Morton Payne and Edward Gilpin as associate editors. With the September 1, 1892 issue the *Dial* became a semimonthly, and its subtitle was "A Semi-Monthly Journal of Literary Criticism, Discussion, and Information." The following year, 1893, Browne established the Dial Press to print books for writers ("authors' editions or private editions"), although his efforts here were modest.

In the October 16, 1882 issue, Browne wrote that the *Dial* was very proud of its distinguished list of contributors, which included former presidents, professors, scholars, and even the current president of the United States, Chester Arthur (No. 3: p. 120). Later, in the 1890s, among his contributors were Woodrow Wilson, Melville B. Anderson, Frederick J. Turner, Katherine Lee Bates, Joseph Jastrow, H.H. Boyesen, W. P. Trent, Richard Henry Stoddard, Fred Lewis Pattee, and Chief Justice Melville W. Fuller.

In 1898 the *Dial* absorbed Herbert S. Stone's *Chap-Book*. Browne's *Dial* before the merger was hostile to the experimental works of its day. It found little to praise in the prose of Stephen Crane and leveled negative criticism again Walt Whitman's poetry. On the other hand, it more than once featured the bad poetry of Harriet Monroe. It was editorially queasy and was against any artistic or intellectual attempt to break with tradition. It took the moral and genteel position when evaluating the worth of American culture. Prior to the merger with the *Dial*, Stone and his assistants, Bliss Carman and Harrison Garfield Rhodes, had published important poets of the day, among them Stephen Crane, W. B. Yeats, and William Vaughn Moody. Among the fictional writers was Thomas Hardy. The spirit of Stone's efforts carried over into the *Dial*. For the first time, because of Stone's interest in experimentation and new writers, the *Dial* showed a variety and aesthetic excitement it had never before possessed. Although Browne had, as late as 1896, told his readers that he had avoided making the magazine physically attractive because he believed that to do so would compromise "the high ideals set for the journal at the start" (No. 20: p. 348), he nevertheless tolerated two years later a relatively radical change in content brought on by Stone's influence. Generally, Browne ran essays and book reviews. Topics usually had to do with literature, history, or some aspect of culture. Regular departments were "Briefs on New Books," "What's in the Magazines," "Trade Book Lists," and "Topics in Leading Periodicals."

Lucian Cary was editor of the *Dial* from October 1913 until February 1915. Only twenty-eight when he took over, Cary was especially interested in the free verses Harriet Monroe was publishing in her magazine *Poetry*. He also gave more attention to "Recent Fiction" than had Browne. But his taste in fiction was, in retrospect, questionable.

Most of the novels he reviewed were of little lasting value, although works by Arnold Bennett, Theodore Dreiser, Louis Couperus, H.G. Wells, and Anatole France were exceptions. Nevertheless, Cary set the magazine on a course toward a position where it would begin to serve the new movements in the arts that had been fermenting in London, Paris, and New York since the turn of the century.

By April 1915, Francis Browne's sons were in charge, Waldo Browne as editor and Herbert S. Browne as president. Frank Luther Mott incorrectly states that Charles Leonard Moore was at this time an associate editor.[1] As editor, Waldo Browne attempted to sustain the publication in the genteel, conservative spirit his father gave it. He brought back William Morton Payne as a contributor as part of this effort, Lucian Cary's influence no doubt being seen as negative. Payne's new presence, as it turned out, was brief. An essay he wrote on German war guilt angered Waldo Browne.[2] Although it was slated for the September 30, 1915 issue, Browne rejected it, and with the rejection, the relationship ended. In some small way, it signaled Herbert Browne's departure from his father's outlook, although the gesture probably is not strong enough to be characterized as a declaration of independence. In June, Waldo Browne moved the magazine from the fashionable Fine Arts Building (where Margaret Anderson's *Little Review* started in 1914) to the Transportation Building at 608 South Dearborn Street.

After Payne's departure, Edward Everett Hale, Jr., who also preferred the consciously polite in literature, wrote the "Recent Fiction" column. For Hale, H.G. Wells was more important than, say, Bernard Shaw. Waldo Browne's sensibility and taste could not have been more compatible with this modest revolt against the so-called vulgar in contemporary literature. Browne was equally closed to what he considered bad taste in painting and the other arts. His *Dial* featured several articles attacking the newer experiments.

However, times were changing, and the *Dial* was losing readers, or certainly not gaining any. After changing it from a semimonthly to a fortnightly in March 1915, the brothers decided to sell. Waldo Browne's last number was the issue of July 15, 1916. Yet, perhaps in spite of himself, Browne made the magazine more specifically literary. Political essays and essays on aspects of society and history of the type his father had published were unacceptable. Perhaps Lucian Cary

influenced Browne's direction. Certainly Browne's social consciousness was every bit as active as his father's had been. But it manifested
itself in a literary way. He was a liberal who supported the efforts of
black people toward full equality. For instance, he published Benjamin
Brawley's "The American Negro in Fiction" in the May 11, 1916 issue
(No. 60: pp. 445-50). This essay attempts to dispel the stereotypical and
propagandistic image of the Negro in contemporary fiction by white
American writers. It was a brave position for Browne at a time when
taking up the cause of the Negro was unpopular. Browne also had
strong feelings about the war. In a review of Romain Rolland's *Above
the Battle* in the March 16, 1916 issue, he spoke out firmly against
nationalism and in favor of human fraternity.

In 1916 Martyn Johnson purchased the Dial Company from the
Brownes. Earlier, Johnson had been involved with the *Trimmed Lamp*.
Its editor, Howard Vincent O'Brien, had started the publication, then
entitled simply *Art*, in October 1912, the same year *Poetry* started, "to
keep the art world of Chicago and the West familiar with what was
going on in the O'Brien art galleries."[3] In March 1914 O'Brien
changed the title to the *Trimmed Lamp* and also opened the pages to
poetry and criticism of the arts. Johnson convinced the editors of and
contributors to the *Trimmed Lamp* to merge the magazine with his. He
also managed to obtain the financial help of Mary L. Snow, Laird Bell,
and Dr. Clinton Masseck. Johnson's takeover was announced to readers of the *Dial* in August 1916. Johnson was listed as the president, and
Masseck was the editor. Masseck's editorship lasted one month.

During this period of upheaval and reorganization, representatives
of the old school and the new movements were published. John Gould
Fletcher wrote for the January 11, 1917 issue a piece entitled "The
Secret of Far Eastern Painting" (No. 62: pp. 3-7), in which he called for
a turning away from such experiments in Europe as cubism toward the
lessons of natural forms in Japanese and Chinese art. In the same number, Richard Aldington's "Poet and Painter: A Renaissance Fancy"
appeared. One might say Fletcher represented the old and Aldington
the new. Among other advocates of the new movements to appear
were Van Wyck Brooks, Maxwell Bodenheim, Babette Deutsch, and a
young Yale man, Henry Seidel Canby, who would later assist Wilbur
Lucius Cross in editing the *Yale Review*. Also included was Amy Lowell.

She was, in a sense, the first to get revenge on Waldo Browne's *Dial* with her essay "In Defense of *Vers Libre*" in August 1916.

Johnson felt completely confident that he had opened his magazine to the spirit and challenge of the contemporary scene. George Bernard Donlin, a graduate of the University of Chicago, was appointed editor, and this was announced in the January 25, 1917 number. In the same column, this statement from the management appeared: "The *Dial* . . . will endeavor to carry on a fruitful tradition . . . to meet the challenge of the new time by reflecting and interpreting its spirit—a spirit freely experimental, skeptical of inherited values, ready to examine old dogmas and to submit afresh its sanctions to the test of experience" (No. 62: p. 37). Poetry, for the first time in seventeen years, began to appear in the pages of the *Dial*. The Johnson *Dial* on the one hand took issue with cubism and futurism, but on the other hand thought Cézanne (the "father" of cubism) a valid, important experimentalist.

Many persons already involved with Johnson's *Dial* would influence cultural tastes through the *Dial* of the 1920s. Among them were Paul Rosenfeld, Gilbert Seldes, James Sibley Watson, Scofield Thayer, and Randolph Bourne. Bourne died from the flu on December 22, 1918, but he became a source of inspiration for Thayer, the future editor of the *Dial*. Late in 1917, Johnson's *Dial* absorbed the *Seven Arts*, a literary monthly that had been published in New York since October 1916. The *Seven Arts* published D. H. Lawrence, Carl Sandburg, Robert Frost, Bourne, Waldo Frank, Van Wyck Brooks, Sherwood Anderson, Eugene O'Neill, and many other new writers. The prestige the *Seven Arts* brought to the *Dial* was undeniable.

Suffering from tuberculosis, Donlin quit the magazine and moved to the West. For a brief period in 1918 the *Dial* had no editor, but then Harold Stearns agreed to act as caretaker and moved from New York to Chicago to take charge. Ironically, the magazine itself moved to New York during July and August, and Stearns, who did not like Chicago, was among many of those happy with the move. The new office opened in an artistically symbolic place—Greenwich Village, at 152 Thirteenth Street.

With the January 11, 1919 issue, Robert Morss Lovett became editor, but the end of Johnson's fortnightly was already in sight. According to S. Foster Damon, Scofield Thayer bought Johnson's magazine in

December 1919.[4] The November 29 issue carried notice of Johnson's resignation (No. 67: p. 486). This same issue announced termination of the entire editorial staff and gave the first public notice that the publication was now owned and managed by Dr. James Sibley Watson, Jr., president, with Scofield Thayer as secretary-treasurer and editor. The new owners announced that the magazine would become a monthly. Thayer had already been an associate editor on Johnson's and Donlin's staff. But now, in their fourth issue of April 1920, they declared that the *Dial* "cannot be everything to everybody. It is non-political and has no message for the million" (No. 68: unnumbered opening page). This amounted to a declaration of independence from the past. Thayer, the guiding force, aimed to publish the best creative and critical works available, but not scientific or sociological essays. He felt that America was stuck in an apathetic, unimaginative state, and in response he would push Bourne's theory of transnationalism, among other ideas.

Although he said politics were out of bounds, before long he used the *Dial* to oppose the activities of the New York Society for the Suppression of Vice, but only because, in his view, it interfered with artistic freedom. (This group brought a lawsuit against Margaret Anderson for publishing an excerpt from James Joyce's *Ulysses.*) Nicholas Joost sees a paradox in the magazine's commitment to both nonpolitical liberalism and pure aesthetics.[5] Although the *Dial* encouraged philosophical argument, it remained stern in its liberal progressive views, in its commitment to aesthetic diversity.

Meanwhile, Thayer, Watson, and Mitchell were publishing the writings of Djuna Barnes, John Dewey, Bertrand Russell, Van Wyck Brooks, Paul Rosenfeld, Sherwood Anderson, e.e. cummings, Marianne Moore, Carl Sandburg, Hart Crane, John Dos Passos, William Carlos Williams, and William Butler Yeats. In 1921 they published T. S. Eliot's "The Waste Land," Ezra Pound's "Cantos," and Thomas Mann's *Death in Venice.* D. H. Lawrence's work, like that of most of those mentioned above, was not then widely known in the United States. In the September 1921 issue, the *Dial* began to publish Lawrence, starting with his story "Adolf." This was followed by the poem "Pomegranate" (March 1921). Excerpts from *Sea and Sardinia* ran in October 1921, and the February 1922 issue carried an excerpt from *Aaron's Rod.* In fact, Lawrence's writings appeared in almost

every issue of the *Dial* until June 1925. In 1922, two years after Martyn
Johnson gave up on the *Dial*, he made an assessment of Lawrence in
a review of *Aaron's Rod* for the *Los Angeles Times* (Sunday), quoted in
the *Dial:* Lawrence was "one of the most important [figures] in the
entire range of literature."[6] Through the *Dial*, Lawrence reached a
larger yet no less sensitive audience than he had previously through
Harriet Monroe's *Poetry* and his books published by Thomas Seltzer.

In addition, wonderful and simple line drawings by e.e. cummings
and Toulouse-Lautrec were reproduced. Reproductions of Picasso's
clowns, Chagall's dream-schemes, Brancusi's sculptures, and the
expressionist art of Bosschere, Hunt Diederich, and Maria Uhden
appeared. Also included were cartoons by William Gropper, pencil or
ink drawings by Beardsley, Gatson Lachaise, Claude Bragdon, Ivan
Opffer, Hildegarde Watson, Richard Boix, Adolf Dehn, Diedrich, and
Max Liebermann, as well as reproductions of woodblock prints by
Uhden, Ann Merrimn Peck, and Frans Masereel.

The departments were no less interesting. The *Dial* commonly
reviewed books such as Irwing Babbitt's *Rousseau and Romanticism*,
Leon Bazalgette's *Walt Whitman: The Man and His Work*, Chekhov's
The Bishop and Other Stories and *The Cherry Orchard*, Chesterton's *Irish
Impressions*, Samuel Langhorne Clemen's *A Double Barrelled Detective
Story—Roughing It—A Tramp Abroad*, and new editions of Walt
Whitman's *Leaves of Grass*. It focused a keen eye on the theater too.
Reviews of *Hamlet, Power of Darkness,* and *Richard the Third*, as well as
productions of newer works such as *Clarence and His Lady Friends*
appeared. Normally, in the departments, there was a "Dublin Letter"
and one from London.

The *Dial* was now firmly joined in the task of achieving a cultural revolution. Thayer could depend on the quality of art and writing in his pages to help achieve the common goals he shared with
Margaret Anderson, editor of the *Little Review,* Gorham B. Munson of
S_4N and *Secession*, Ford Madox Ford of the *Transatlantic Review,* Ezra
Pound in London and Paris, Eugene Jolas and Elliot Paul of *transition*,
and others committed to the struggle. By maintaining high standards
and putting out an attractive, appealing magazine, Thayer moved the
Dial quickly to the forefront, and, by 1925, when Marianne Moore
replaced him as editor, the magazine had been established as a trend-

setter, a cultural institution, and, for some, a work of art itself. The year before Thayer left, the staff established the Dial Press.

Marianne Moore continued in the direction set by Thayer and his coeditors and assistants. In 1927 a Dial Award was created, and the first one, announced in the issue of January 1928, was given to Pound. The issue also carried T. S. Eliot's enthusiastic review of Pound's *Personae*, originally published in London in 1909, and drawings by Pound's friend and coeditor of *Blast* (1914-1915), Wyndham Lewis. H.D., who had also been close to Pound, had her *Hippolytus Temporizes* reviewed here. This was a very special issue for Pound.

By 1929, when so many cultural forces were squashed by the world economic crisis, the *Dial* had already served its purpose well. Along with the *Little Review* and the other journals of the arts and literature, it had introduced to an astonished world the art of the twentieth century. The *Dial* was forced to fold because of money problems.

The role the *Dial* played in presenting, preserving, and advancing the new literature is enormous. Any assessment of modern literature in English would be incomplete without an acknowledgement of that role.

CONSIDERING THE *YALE REVIEW*

During its first years as an independent magazine (1892–1911), the *Yale Review* was controlled by Henry Farnam, son-in-law of Congregational minister William L. Kingsley, who had edited the earlier *New Englander and Yale Review.* Kingsley's journal was heavily slanted toward the propagation of religious dogma. Farnam shifted the focus in his magazine to theories and problems of economics, political arguments, and social issues, especially in Europe.

Farnam's vision of a successful society involved keeping government out of industry and business. His contributors—most of them professors at Yale—either supported Farnam's conservative philosophy or at least did not express opposing views. Nevertheless, the *Yale Review*'s subtitle, "A Quarterly Journal of History and Political Science," which in May 1896 became "A Quarterly Journal for Scientific Discussion of Economic, Political and Social Questions," was meant to suggest that the magazine had no special commitment to a particular party or school. The *Review*'s pages were filled with articles such as "Wealth and Moral Law," "Capital Interest," "Philosophy and Political Economy," "Socialism and Social Reform," "The Sphere of the State," "Social Evolution," "A Student's Manual of English Constitutional History," and "Money and Monetary Problems." In retrospect, it might seem that only the ads supplied variety and some welcome comic relief: "A Tonic / For Brain Workers, / The Weak and Debilitated. / Horsford's Acid Phosphate / is without exception" (Vol. 3: No. 1).

In the unsigned "Comment," Farnam and his editors preached wearisome sermons on the same subjects. For example, "There are only two ways to estimate the actual effect of a tariff bill on the rate duty. One is to take the various imports under the bill previously existing, and by laborious calculation to find what would be the duty on the same articles under the new bill" (Vol. 1: No. 235). The August 1903 "Comment" explored "Economics and the Papacy . . ." with a focus on Pope Leo XIII's condemnation of "socialism, communists, and nihilists" (Vol. 2: No. 8). The "Comment" notes that even though the Pope first spoke out against socialism in 1878, it had "grown steadily" (Vol. 2: No. 8). This sort of concern for the effects of one area of life on another is characteristic of this early period.

Between May 1903 and February 1904, the *Yale Review* gave much of its space to such questions as: "Suffrage and Self-Government in Puerto Rico," "A Sociological View of the Native Question," "The Northern Interest in the Negro Problem," and "The Financial Versus the Industrial History of the Country." Although Farnam's influence as an economist was still dominant, intellectuals from other disciplines clearly were having an effect on contents. But they were not from widely diverse areas of study or of the country. Still mostly Yale professors, they agreed to work with Farnam without pay. In 1896, two of those who had started out with Farnam, George Burton Adams, whose specialty was religion, and George Park Fisher, who taught European history, left the *Review*. At the same time, Edward Gaylord Bourne and Irving Fisher joined. Arthur T. Hadley, who was an associate from the beginning, continued to write on economic theory. Both Clive Day and Albert Calloway Keller started in 1902 and were joined by Henry Crosby Emery by 1903.[1] John Christopher Schwab, the managing editor who had started out with Farnam, was on the staff at least until 1904. Similarly, William Fremont Blackman, interested in social issues, was also one of Farnam's feature writers and reviewers.

With these new contributors there seemed to be a widening of interest. Reading from volumes 9 through 13, one has no difficulty imagining the editors making a conscious effort to reach a larger audience. For example, volume 9 (May 1900 through February 1901) includes Clive Day's two articles "Experience of the Dutch with Tropical Labor," as well as Albert G. Keller's many contributions on such varied subjects as Italy, the Netherlands, France, Sweden, nobility, waterways, and colonies. Nevertheless, although the stated objective of these Yale professors was to open the *Review* to more diverse thought, there was—judging from the *Review's* still very formal and sober contents—little chance of its reaching a wide lay audience beyond the faculty and other intellectuals on its subscriber list. In addition, its limited readership was due in good part to lack of finances and distribution facilities. Mott himself describes all the early Farnam issues as "pretty dull."[2] He implies, moreover, that this dullness coupled with the pressure of competition finally forced Farnam to fold. This competition stemmed from, among other sources, the fact that the American Economic Association produced a journal of its own, the *American Economic Review*, beginning in 1911. Wilbur Lucius Cross, the next editor of the *Yale Review*, later wrote: "By 1880 the general interest in theology was fast waning," which led to the end of the *New Englander* and the birth of Farnam's magazine. Now, because of Farnam's "restricted . . . program," the *Yale Review* "soon developed trouble similar to that which Kingsley had experienced with theology."[3]

Given a free hand by the president of Yale University, Cross, an English professor and Laurence Sterne scholar, became the editor of the *Yale Review* in 1911. Cross was attracted to the idea of having his own magazine: "I could publish anything I might write."[4] But it would be more than a personal vehicle. His first number appeared in October, and for the first time the *Yale Review* showed signs of having a national character. Cross's objective was to publish articles of exceptional quality in literature, art, history, religion, public issues, and the social and natural sciences: "I thought of it . . . as a quarterly addressed to . . . the mature mind . . . it would be cultural and educative . . . yet good reading . . . it would give scope and leeway for the free play of the creative intelligence." His literary views were liberal: "One of the most important services an editor can render to his readers is to keep the road open for candid statements of different standpoints from writers of exceptional ability."[5] He aimed at making his theme "The United States in relation to all nations of the earth." Fortunately he had help from two of his former students, Henry Seidel Canby and Edward Bliss Reed. His business manager was Edwin Oviatt. Cross described his staff and himself as amateurs: "We had to work out our salvation without the aid of experts."[6]

The fact that Cross was lucky or clever enough to secure manuscripts from well-known authors (William Graham Sumner, William

H. Taft, Gilbert Murray, Virginia Woolf, John Galsworthy, H. G. Wells, André Maurois) soon helped to place the publication in not only a national but also an international arena. Edith Wharton wrote on Proust, and Gertrude Atherton discussed "The Woman of Tomorrow." Henry Adams sent Cross a long poem inspired by "the sacred Bo-tree of Buddha" while in Ceylon. The sophisticated cartoons of Max Beerbohm added humor. The cartoons were symptomatic of the sense of humor Cross expressed in his role as editor. "A Boston woman, it was reported to me, remarked that she had to read every word, covers and all, as the magazine cost so much."[7] Cross did not take his editorship so seriously as to miss the opportunity for fun. Yet, he not only made lively and intelligent editorial decisions, but he also contributed criticism to the *Review*, focusing primarily on contemporary fiction. Earlier, as a student of Kingsley, he had written a critique of Ibsen that appeared in the *New Englander* and *Yale Review*.

Apparently, without the untiring assistance of Helen MacAfee, who joined the staff in 1912,[8] Cross could not have made the journal the success that it became. When he resigned on January 1, 1940, she took full control. Her new editorial board consisted of several deans and professors at Yale. However, the *Yale Review* continued its previous policies, tone, and diversity. Her presence, it is safe to assume, had found expression in the magazine long before 1940. MacAfee earned Cross's respect: "To her breadth of knowledge and fine literary sense the *Yale Review* was immensely indebted during my editorship . . . nothing pertaining to human culture seemed to be alien to her mind. Without her devoted aid, I should have been compelled to forgo many other enterprises."[9]

Poetry first appeared in the *Review* during Cross's years as editor. However, his and apparently MacAfee's tastes in "verse" were a bit conservative. Works by John Crowe Ransom (of the Fugitives), Amy Lowell (so-called sponsor of the imagists), Edgar Lee Masters, Witter Bryner, and Edwin Arlington Robinson were published. The more radical poets of vers libre—Pound, Eliot, Williams, cummings—did not appear. Cross and MacAfee's policy regarding fiction, when the magazine started running it in 1930, was not as restrained. Works by William Saroyan, with their lightness and special humor, appeared with stories by Kay Boyle, Walter Van Tilburg

Clark, and Dorothy Canfield. Many British and other foreign fiction
writers were also represented.

Although Cross was still listed as editor in chief, MacAfee carried
the *Review* through the 1940s. She was replaced in 1949 and became
editor emeritus. The next editor in chief was David Morris Potter, a
historian specializing in the American experience. Potter's managing
editor was an English professor, Paul Pickrel, who started with him
and continued in the same position after Potter's editorship ended in
1954. That year, John James Ellis Palmer took over. Palmer continued
the tradition set by Cross and MacAfee, as the September 1954 issue
demonstrates. It contains Dean Acheson's "The Responsibility for
Decision in Foreign Policy," E. B. White's "Walden—1954," and
Herbert Gold's "Americans in Port of Princes." Although there are no
longer as many reviews, the types of books selected for review are the
same (on Kierkegaard, on economics, on science, for example). Pickrel
writes a roundup of current fiction, but the "Comment" column of
Farnam's day is gone. Archibald T. MacAllister writes on "The
Literature of Italy," and Saroyan, then very popular, has another story
here. Nine years later, in the December 1963 issue, the *Review* is still
dominated by essays on politics, social issues, and economics. Although
it is not as restricted as it had been in the past, especially under
Farnam, it is safely attempting not to be all things to all people. This
particular issue carries one story and several poems. (Poetry in these
years, as in the past, is characterized as "verse," and no more than two
or three such works appear per issue.) Robert Penn Warren's prose
"All the King's Men: The Matrix of Experience" is the lead piece, and
now, for the first time, film and record reviews are run at the end of
the magazine. Palmer's editorship ended in 1979. Cleanth Brooks
wrote the tribute to him, which led the October 1979 issue. In it,
Brooks said, "I welcome the opportunity to salute . . . Palmer. . . . He
is a remarkable person. . . . These last unbroken years as editor have had
their complexities, for complexity is a built-in character of our friend"
(Vol. 69: p. ii). With this issue, Kai T. Erikson became editor and Sheila
Huddleston managing editor.

Erikson's editorship seems to have involved a conscious effort to
reconnect with and sustain the past temperament, tone, and taste of the
Review. The "Comment" department was, for example, reinstituted in

the July 1983 issue. In reading the issues since Erikson's beginning issue, one finds the dominant concern to be with historical criticism, literary theory, modernism, and poetry. (In fact, more space is given to poetry than ever before.) Volume 69, for example, includes essays on or reviews of books concerned with Edmund Spenser, Nietzsche, Rainer Maria Rilke, Marcel Proust, Ezra Pound, Jacques Derrida, Byron, Keats, Samuel Johnson, Mary Wollstonecraft, the Puritans, the Quakers, Lewis Carroll, Herman Melville, Marx, Shakespeare, and Roman history. A few contemporary creative works are also reviewed.

There are some differences between Erikson's policies and the policies of Palmer. Erikson states, "Palmer . . . rarely solicited material, while we print many more solicited articles than submitted ones." Erikson, a member of the Yale sociology faculty, was asked to edit the magazine "in the hope that I would broaden its scope . . . introducing more political commentary and social analysis. . . . That has proven difficult, in part because my own interests have always been quite humanistic and in part because a considerable majority of the submissions we receive in the mail are literary in content." Erikson continues, "We have tried . . . to avoid the kind of literary criticism that seems to be addressed to other members of the guild, and we have managed to attract a fair number of authors who speak of more general matters in a more general tone of voice."[10] In addition, poets now serve as the poetry editors. J. D. McClatchy served from 1980 to 1982 and William Meredith has served since.

Erikson also has the assistance of associate editor Penelope Laurans, who is a specialist in twentieth-century poetry: "She has networks that reach out into the literary world, while I have networks reaching out elsewhere; and the two of us, in collaboration with a board of advisors with whom we meet occasionally, do most of the soliciting." Erikson adds:

> If I have an operating philosophy in the way I treat the
> magazine, it is that our readers should be exposed to
> material of real intelligence from a variety of intellec-
> tual sources, and that those who write for us should
> always address themselves to audiences of thoughtful
> generalists rather than to audiences of disciplinary

peers. This is a hard policy to maintain . . . not only because authors are never quite certain where that murky border is located, but because editors are full of uncertainties on the matter as well.[11]

The *Yale Review*, now calling itself "A National Quarterly," has compromised none of its earlier objectives.

One is tempted to think of institutional backing as both a blessing and a curse. *Yale Review*, of course, cannot be separated from the image of Yale University. More conservative perhaps because of traditional backing than, say, the *Dial* or the *Little Review*, it nevertheless was a remarkable and innovative forum and, in its own way, helped establish the modern literature of the twentieth century.

THE *LITTLE REVIEW* IN FOCUS

I n 1906, at the age of twenty, Margaret Anderson left Columbus, Indiana to escape family control.[1] Although she said she was twenty-one when she decided to start the *Little Review* (p. 35), the decision was made either late in 1913 or early in 1914 when she was twenty-seven. The first issue appeared that year in March. Between 1906, the year she left Western College for Women in Oxford, Ohio and 1914, she lived in Chicago. She wrote book reviews until 1912,[2] when she secured a job earning eight dollars per week working as a clerk in Francis F. Browne's *Dial* bookshop. For two months, in Browne's shop and the printing office at the same location in the Fine Arts Building, she learned editing, proofreading, and copyediting, becoming familiar with the language of the typesetting room. She also assisted Browne in editing the *Dial,* but she left his employ because of his unwelcome advances.[3]

Described by Bernard Duffey as possessing a "double quality of unreality . . . one part outward, the other within," Margaret Anderson was unquestionably a remarkable person in many ways. Foremost she was sensitively intelligent: "I demand that life be inspired every moment" (p. 35). Duffey's point about her outward beauty ("Golden hair and unearthly blue eyes"[4]) is evident in her photographs; her inward singularity is proven by her eccentric writings and the excellent taste she showed as an editor and lover of art.

Anderson returned to work in 1913 for the religious magazine *Continent* (for which she had worked briefly upon her arrival in Chicago) because it would offer her the chance to travel often to New York to interview publishers about forthcoming books.[5] Refusing to denounce Theodore Dreiser's novel *Sister Carrie* as sinful, Anderson was fired by the editor of the *Continent* after only a short time. Although she valued the book, Anderson was impatient with its author: "Dreiser had no more wit than a cow." She declared that she could "only talk to people who love talk for its own sake" (p. 39).

When it came, Anderson's own magazine was an expression of herself—a "personal enterprise" (Vol. 1: No. 2). In her need for "inspired conversation," she started the *Little Review* to have it "every moment" (p. 35). At Floyd Dell's literary salon, she began telling everyone that she was "about to publish the most interesting magazine that had ever been launched" (p. 35). Among those listening were Sherwood Anderson, John Cowper Powys, Arthur Davidson Ficke, Edna Kenton, Llewellyn Jones, Jerome Blum, George Cram Cook, Susan Glaspell, and Dreiser. Later, many of them became her contributors. Soon she raised $450 and got the support of DeWitt C. Wing, a "friend-suitor" she met through Dell.[6] Wing edited an agricultural publication, the *Breeder's Gazette:* "He was one of those civilized men . . . more interested in an idea than in a woman" (p. 39). Anderson opened her office in "one of the most delightful buildings in the world," the Chicago Fine Arts Building (p. 45).

The first issue of the *Little Review* contained poetry by Rupert Brooke, Ficke, and Vachel Lindsay, as well as articles by George Soule, George Burman Foster, and Anderson herself. It was an impressive beginning: sixty-four pages with seventeen pages of advertising, six inches by nine inches: "A temple . . . not the petite chapelle" (p. 46). Dell reviewed it in his column for the *Chicago Evening Post,* which greatly helped sales.

The second and third numbers drew the support of a number of other Chicagoans, among them poet Eunice Strong Tietjens and architect Frank Lloyd Wright. Offended by Anderson's praise of feminist Emma Goldman in the third issue dated May 1914, DeWitt withdrew his support. Amy Lowell, who earlier had tried to buy her way into a controlling editorial position on Harriet Monroe's *Poetry,* offered to help Anderson financially in exchange for an appointment as poetry editor. Anderson refused. The second issue is especially important for William Butler Yeats's speech addressed to American poets in which he describes the formation of the Rhymer's Club "to strip away everything that was artificial, to get a style like speech" (p. 51). In later issues Anderson "toned down somewhat her desperate ardor for art, influenced not only by the letters of criticism that poured in [printed in number 2] but also by . . . too-sentimental congratulations" (p. 52). Goldman's influence, however, remained, showing its effects in the issues for the next two years. As Anderson lost subscribers, Goldman became an ever-closer friend.

Anderson struggled financially in 1915 and 1916. When she could not pay her rent, she (with her sister Lois, Lois's "two exceptional children" [p. 80], and Harriet "Deansie" Dean and her two children) pitched tents in the spring on the beach between Braeside and Highland Park. They lived in them as an act of protest as well as to live "the pristine life of nomads" (p. 86). Sherwood Anderson came out to enjoy the campfire and tell them stories. Margaret Anderson's gypsy life lasted for six months. In addition to loving art for itself, she now fell in love with nature. A few concerned readers and other sympathizers sent her small sums to help. Poets left poems pinned on her tent door. While she was "growing" as a feminist, a supporter of innovations in the arts, and an anarchist, her family back in Indiana thought she was crazy. "If anyone should ever ask me what I consider the most wearing experience known to mankind . . . I will answer: waiting for other people to act upon what I see" (p. 86).

Over the years Anderson got to know many of her contributors, and, though she was soon competing with magazines such as the *Dial* that could pay, she got from her friends some of their best works. In the first issue, Sherwood Anderson wrote "The New Note." He began: "The new note in the craft of writing is in danger, as are all new and beautiful things born into the world." This was a "cry for the reinjection of truth and honesty into the craft." It was also a clear manifesto for those writers Margaret Anderson was defending by publishing their works, when most of them were being rejected by commercial publishers. In addition to Sherwood Anderson himself, these writers included Ezra Pound, T. S. Eliot, Vachel Lindsay, James Joyce, Witter Bynner, Lola Ridge, Gertrude Stein, Djuna Barnes, Wallace Stevens, Malcolm Cowley, William Carlos Williams, Richard Aldington, William Butler Yeats, Hart Crane, Guillaume Apollinaire, Wyndham Lewis, Edgar Lee Masters, H. D., Amy Lowell, Carl Sandburg, and Ford Madox Ford. Goldman's letters from prison began to appear in 1916. She had been imprisoned, according to Anderson, "for advocating that 'women need not always keep their mouths shut and their wombs open.'" In one letter Goldman wrote, "My only consolation is that the fight is not at an end."[7]

In the early spring of 1916, Anderson met Jane Heap, who was to become her companion and associate editor until 1924. Heap had been an art student, and her drawings occasionally appeared in the *Little Review* along with her editorial comments and other writings. Later in 1916, the two companions moved to California, where, in September, they published their most infamous issue, sixty-four blank pages, the result of not having received anything worth printing. The exception was a centerfold of cartoons by Heap of Anderson engaged in humorous episodes of her life—at breakfast, suffering for humanity at an Emma Goldman lecture, gathering her own firewood, at the piano, and so on.

The California period was short-lived. Early the next year Anderson and Heap moved the *Little Review* to New York. Ezra Pound, in a letter written from London in April 1916, had already agreed to serve as foreign editor.[8] The magazine was about to enter its most intense and fascinating period. In another letter dated January 1917 Pound said, "The *Little Review* is perhaps temperamentally closer to what I want done?????? . . . I want an 'official organ' (vile phrase). I mean I want a place where I and T. S. Eliot can appear once a month (or once an 'issue') and where Joyce can appear when he likes, and where Wyndham Lewis can appear if he comes back from the war."[9] Later, in May, Pound encouraged Anderson to tolerate the lawyer and art patron John Quinn. In the issue for May 1917, Pound defended his "right" to serve on the *Little Review* without resigning from Harriet Monroe's *Poetry*. Meanwhile, he continued to blast off angry letters to Anderson on a variety of literary issues and people, among them what made a good poem, who was good, who was not.

With the March 1918 number, Joyce's *Ulysses* began to appear serially. It ran for three years. Anderson was convinced she and Heap were publishing "the most beautiful thing we'll ever have!"[10] Heap later wrote, "Issues were held up by the post office and destroyed, we were tried and fined for sections of the book." John Quinn defended the two editors in the Court of Special Sessions. After all the trouble they were fined only one hundred dollars. However, as Heap observed, none of New York's intellectuals came to the defense of Joyce's brilliant work, nor to that of the *Little Review.*[11]

During the next three years Anderson was understandably depressed: "I didn't know what to do about life—so I did a nervous breakdown that lasted many months." She considered folding the *Review*. When in 1921 she met the French singer Georgette Leblanc (who was in New York at the time), Anderson even considered taking seriously Leblanc's proposal that they work together, with Anderson as pianist. The idea of touring Europe with Leblanc appealed to her. "In late 1922 or early 1923," Anderson, Heap, and Leblanc went by ship to France.[12] In Paris they met Pound for the first time. Very soon Anderson and Heap had met the expatriate literary colony that centered itself around Sylvia Beach's bookshop, Shakespeare & Company. Among them were Hemingway, Joyce, Gertrude Stein, and the composer George Antheil. By 1914, Jane Heap sailed for New York taking the *Little Review* with her. Leblanc and Anderson remained idealistic: "I was naïve enough to think that people could be changed by listening to great theories ... Georgette and I had faith in these illusions and ... Jane had not."[13]

From 1924 to 1927, Heap put out the *Little Review* from her New York art gallery at 66 Fifth Avenue, continuing it as a quarterly and changing it little. Margaret Anderson, who felt she had done her part for the new literature, remained in Europe. She and Georgette Leblanc lived together, mostly in the south of France, for the next twenty-one years in "absolute perfection."[14] As the magazine neared its end in 1929, Jane Heap sent out a questionnaire to its writers. Among the questions was: "What do you look forward to?"[15] In a way, the *Little Review* helped to create the means for greater public acceptance of the modernist writers by its sustained presence and support, by its look forward into the future.

READING WILLIAM FAULKNER'S
LIGHT IN AUGUST

". . . to create out of the materials of the human spirit
something which did not exist before."
—WILLIAM FAULKNER

Sometimes William Faulkner's fiction conjures up for me images akin to those found in, say, the paintings of Edvard Munch. Both painter and writer share a particular kind of cold and cold-blooded angst. Munch's 1901 lithograph "Dead Lovers," which depicts a man and a woman lying dead on a stark bed, blood running down from the mattress to the floor, might have served as a jacket illustration for *Light in August* (1932).

Although first read more than twenty years ago, *Light in August* is one of the few novels whose scenes have stayed with me, I think primarily because I find three of the five or six main characters in this complex, third-person narrative—Joe Christmas, Joanna Burden, and Lena Grove—so unforgettable. And they live in my mind as *characters,* not symbols—though they generate much symbolism.

The story of Lena Grove (the fertility implication in the last name is not to be missed) is running side by side with that of Joe Christmas. One of the main surface connections between Joe and Lena is that established by Joe's senile grandmother who, due to confusion, has decided that Lena is Milly (her daughter), the biological mother of Joe and the daughter of (her husband) the crazy old Doc Hines, Joe's maternal grandfather. Although Lena and Joe have come to Jefferson, a relatively small Mississippi community, their paths never cross during the several months duration of the novel's action.

Although Joe and Lena never meet, and have no practical reason to, their stories are also connected by other ironic threads: Lena arrives in town and immediately establishes her presence while Joe has been in Jefferson three years and still has none; because she's pregnant, Lena can be read as a bringer of life, while Joe harbors and carries the blueprint for his own symbolic demise and actual death; Lena is searching for something—fulfillment, a husband?—and Joe is fleeing something—his own invalidated and undefined self. These two are also connected through Joe's bunkmate, Joe Brown, the runaway father of Lena's unborn child.

Joe Christmas doesn't know whether he's black or white in a community where, arguably, being one or the other—where race—matters more than anything else. Joe might be seen as a racialized sacrificial figure, and if looked at in that way, he can be said to represent the main social and moral plight of the Old South, the New South, and perhaps the whole country, past and present. Because of the moral history of his region, Joe can also be seen narrowly in the context of a Puritan system of thought. The same is true of Joanna Burden, the white woman who employs Joe and whom he eventually murders.

Following this line of thought, one could argue, as some critics have, that Joanna Burden carries the burden of liberal guilt for the legacy of slavery. But the irony of her position, in her relation with Joe, is striking, because from Joe's point of view, being either white or black becomes unacceptable. He eventually defies the American pathology of *race naming*, which I believe is one of the primary causes of American racism.

At the same time, Joe is the ultimate force of self denial. In the beginning, he is the victim of a cruel and vicious misunderstanding. Left as an infant on the doorstep of an orphanage, he begins to grow up, and one day when he's five, he is caught by the dietician eating toothpaste. The act itself becomes a personal legacy he must carry all his life because, rather than punishing him for something he himself felt to be wrong, the dietician instead attempts to buy his silence—incorrectly assuming that the boy has been witness to her clandestine encounter with a man in her room.

In the meantime, the narrative tone and slant seem to suggest that Joe, as a result of the encounter with the dietician, later in life cannot tolerate the idea of food (which can be read as a symbolic rejection of life itself) although he must eat to live. In fact, all the needs of the body and the spirit are forces he is at war with. Joe eventually has sex with Joanna Burden, but there seems to be only torment in the guilty passion generated between them.

Intimacy, love, warmth, romance, caring, are all totally repulsive to Joe. Early on, his first sexual encounter is with a "Negro" girl in a toolshed. Rebelling against the white South's male custom of initiation into sex by way of the black woman, he attacks the girl and the other white boys who wish to have sex with her. Further, when Joe discovers that women shed blood periodically, he goes out and kills a sheep so that he can bathe his hands in the blood of the lamb, so to speak. This Old Testament ceremony is not Faulkner's only biblical reference. When his foster mother, Mrs. McEachern, washes his feet, the correlation to Christ is obvious. Although Faulkner himself denied that there was any intended biblical analogies, the name Christmas, and Joe's "birth" date—December twenty-fifth—are enough to justify reading the string of correlations as biblical analogies.

Abstinence—from food, sex, etc.—is associated in Joe's mind with masculinity and manhood. From the very beginning, he seems to have a sense of the betrayal and the execution awaiting him in the near future. At one point, Joe could see himself floating away as pure air, a moment that foreshadows his death. By the time he takes up with Joanna his days are numbered. Joe's brief encounter with the Reverend Gail Hightower has already foreshadowed this, as has his relationship with the no-account drifter, Joe Brown (also known as Lucas Burch).

Faulkner's novel can also be read, in its main thrust, as a critique of the moral influence of the Puritans on southern Protestant Christianity. The key voice representing this posture is that of the Reverend Gail Hightower, who denounces his fellow townsmen because they cannot "bear" pleasure or "ecstasy." Hightower: "And so why should not their [his neighbors'] religion drive them to crucifixion of themselves and one another?"

Hightower's indictment of southern Puritanism and perversions of Christianity might be seen as Faulkner's most direct rejection of their component mythic stance, fanatical white supremacy. But to believe this one would have to be convinced that Faulkner shared Hightower's position. It's true though that Hightower expresses despair in the face of the grim fundamentalist racist community of which he himself—like Faulkner—is part. At the same time, Hightower is the only character who expresses sympathy with and finally pity for Joe. On the other hand, Joanna's interest in Joe cannot be described as purely sympathetic. Also, unlike the third-person narrative voice of the implied author, Hightower refuses to see Joe as a sacrificial figure. It is to his credit that he doesn't, and it is precisely because Joe is *not* a Christ figure (but, hypothetically, in almost any other context, a "regular" human being) that Hightower sympathizes with and feels sorry for him. Gods and saviors don't need the pity of men and women.

The proof of Joe's down-to-earth humanity is all over the place. In terms of behavior, he is cocky and arrogant. Like so many other uneducated, rural drifters, Joe is suspicious of strangers, and a man of few words. To disguise his own chaos or emptiness, he wears a poker face. The point is, Joe is not solely a freak product of his culture, as so many critics have argued: he is easy to locate, and this is Hightower's point, and one of the causes of the minister's despair. Ironically, in terms of culturally shaped personality, Joe could easily be one in a lynch mob about to string up a guilty or innocent Negro for sport, just like many of the other "white" young men in Jefferson. The ambiguity of Joe's so-called negative "racial" identity—always there, though at times subtextually—does not alter entirely what he shares culturally with the Puritan Christian community of which he is a product. In fact, I would argue that he has more in common with these people (who would reject him) than he has with what potentially separates him.

On the other hand, Joanna Burden is as deeply subject to the Puritan code as is Joe Christmas, but by nightfall she is, at least on the surface, a whirlwind of sexual passion. Juxtaposed to this activity she begs Joe to pray with her for forgiveness. The two separate acts begin to constitute a ritual. Consequently, Joe begins to hate Joanna as much as he hated his foster mother and Bobbie his first (white) girlfriend. He especially hates those who love or try to love him. They seem to defy or defeat his primary mission, which is both an intricate, common, and intrinsic blending of the will to survive and a drive toward self-destruction. His hatred for women equals his self-hatred and his hatred of both white and black people. Both forms of hatred are connected and have the same roots.

Although one might make an argument in favor of the mirroring effects of Joe and Joanna, the case is not especially interesting to me. Of far more interest is the case of how they differ. Although Joe's encounter with Joanna—and her death—show him more about himself (in all of his bleakness) than any other experience with another human being has, he has no way to put the knowledge to use and to change his deterministic outlook and fate. Joanna, on the other hand, has had her fling and now retreats to her harsh, repenting, and repressive way of life, especially now that she has entered what she thinks of as the so-called "change" of life.

The crisis is also intensified if not triggered by Joanna Burden's plan to send Joe to a Negro college—essentially a "normal" school. Although she means well, Joe cannot accept her definition of him as "colored." But her liberalism and the history of her good efforts on behalf of Negroes leaves her with no other choice. Given her convictions, it is her personal means to salvation.

Not surprisingly—in theory, at least—together she and Joe find a way to resolve this conflict. So loaded with guilt still, she comes close to getting Joe to agree to a double suicide. After she attempts to shoot him, he lets her have it with a knife. In terms of the novel's plot, this act seals Joe's death-fate even tighter and points the way toward his redemption. In addition to the legal and moral nature of this act of murder, such a plot device as this is given additional grim weight by the sexualized racial history of the region.

Joe's flight, whether or not Faulkner intended it, can be read as an indictment of the southern legal definition of race and color cast, and as an indictment of the racial legacy of the South generally, especially since it is while in flight that Joe achieves a kind of social wisdom, if not a spiritual delivery from his own emptiness and chaos. Essentially, while in flight, Joe has figured out the bogus nature of race itself without fully articulating it as such, and by so doing he comes to make sense of himself, validates himself as he is, and rejects permanently the racial pathology of the country when he decides not *ever* to be white or black.

But given its history and how it uses the myth of race, Joe's country cannot accept his validation of himself as a non-racialized being. With nowhere else to go, and given this insight, for Joe, death will be a form of salvation. But first, as if to test his own resolve, he makes a real and symbolic trek through "white" town, then one through "black" town, and discovers that his mind is not changed. Instead, Joe becomes even more set on his destiny of death as the only way out of the racialized world into which he was born.

Joe finally surrenders in a Negro town after exchanging his shoes for those of a Negro woman. Earlier at Mottstown, he had burst into a Negro church and in the pulpit damned the Christian God the colored folk were busy worshipping. The congregation escapes his wrath unharmed. Although Joe appears here in an aggressive manner, the essential thrust of his aggression is directed both at the abstraction of theology—not at the Negroes themselves, as some critics have argued—and inwardly at his own newly affirmed self—a self that, nevertheless, and in practical terms, has no place yet to *be*.

But it is hard to know for sure Faulkner's position, if any, on any moral point concerning Joe Christmas. Yet there is no question that Faulkner understood his character completely, at least as a southern "type." Joe is so much a product of the Puritan South that he cannot envision any moral judgment but fire-and-brimstone justice—even for himself—and of course, at least in literary terms, this sort of justice is precisely the prescriptive plot device Faulkner needed to open and close the scene of Joe's death.

After being chased and castrated by a mob of white men (perhaps more angry because of [black?] Joe's sexual relations with [white] Joanna than because of his killing of her), Joe Christmas, after a long flight, dies on the floor in Reverend Hightower's home. From the reverend's point of view, at the moment of death, Joe's spirit seems to ascend, suggesting that in death he achieves the vindication of divine delivery.

Joe Christmas, then, is in many ways like Melville's Ahab, in that he insists on *his own* final "truth" at any cost. Also, like Ahab, Christmas would rather die than hide behind the safety of a façade—such as *whiteness* or *blackness*. In Joe's case, choosing to be black or white would have meant living the lie of wearing a false mask. So, in the end, he is transformed from the question mark he starts out being, even perhaps transformed from being mainly a local drifter and farmworker, by being made more positive through his own new resolution concerning—and acceptance of—the absence of a racial identity.

In the end, it is not Joe Brown whom Lena finds but the good, simple Byron Bunch, a part-time preacher and millworker, a man of good faith and goodwill. There is, I believe, less uncertainty about the meaning of Lena than there is about Joe. She seems to represent what Faulkner might have described as true Christian virtues, among them love and faith. Faulkner also seems to draw a healthy correlation between Lena and the regenerative seasonal cycles.

At the same time, Lena's future mate, Byron, is Hightower's only real friend. Byron seems to understand how and why Hightower's idealism and abstract approach to life keep him removed from his community in Jefferson. The two men, after all, share an interest in things spiritual. Acting self-consciously as a Christian and a minister, Byron befriends the eccentric, isolated minister the way he might any other unhappy person. He has a way of reaching out to the lost.

It's possible, finally, to find many kinds of symbolic meanings or to draw biblical analogies while exploring *Light in August*. Some critics have seen in the novel the message that suffering is universal, played out in the implied relationship between Joe and Lena as two individual characters who carry different kinds of burdens or crosses. Other critics have seen a struggle between time and space in the way the novel spreads itself out—in a limited way—both in time and geographically. Still others see Joe and Lena as representing the opposing forces in Nature—though in a way that reaffirms Nature's variables and digressions.

Finally, Faulkner is careful to adjust his third-person points-of-view to each of the main characters he happens to be focused on in any given section, as he orchestrates the novel. For my money, it is the complexity of Faulkner's points-of-view, and how that network of *narrowly represented* voices corresponds to, and sets up, a tension with the plot, and its deeply realized characters, that I find so fascinating.

PART THREE: REVIEWING

BLACK AND WHITE IN COLOR

Cambridge, by Caryl Phillips, Knopf, 1992

What is formally most interesting about Caryl Phillips's fourth novel, *Cambridge,* is the contrast between a British white woman's view of slavery and a black slave's. Framed with a brief, third-person prologue and an epilogue, both stories are told in journal form, hers taking the first two-thirds of the novel and his the last third. Both are parodies—hers of the nineteenth-century proper lady's travelogue, while his takes an ironic twist on the slave narrative.

Emily Cartwright, 30 years old, is visiting her father's sugar plantation on an island in the West Indies for the first time. An indirect benefactor of the system, she is making her first direct contact with it. She arrives without any definite ideas about black people or the white men who drive them.

Although she is appalled by much of what she sees, she departs convinced that God made blacks to work for the benefit of whites. Unable to comprehend the negative effects of slavery on both slave and slaveholder, she is convinced it is his contact with the slaves that causes the otherwise good Christian white man to behave in repulsive ways.

Much earlier, but long after England has banned the slave trade, the African Olumide is kidnapped at the age of 15 and taken aboard a slave ship headed for the Americas. The captain takes a liking to him and renames him Tom, like a pet, and keeps him. Tom grows up in his master's Pall Mall mansion in London and under the guidance of his teacher, Miss Spencer, becomes a devout Christian and later an unsuccessful proselytizer.

An English gentleman of color, he renames himself David Henderson and marries his master's maid. After Tom's English wife,

Anna, dies in childbirth, he sets out for Africa intending to convert his
"uncivilized" former countrymen. But before he reaches the continent
of his birth, he is betrayed by the ship's captain and ends up, this time for
good, a slave in the West Indies. The overseer renames him Cambridge,
presumably because he has such a terrific command of English.

When Emily arrives at her father's plantation, Cambridge is
already an old man who has felt the impact of years of joyless toil. The
ironic and sharply contrasting views of the white woman and the slave
suggest that they both have been duped. She is blind to the true nature
of the system she has bought into, and so is he. But he is doubly blind
because he has taken to heart the teachings of the very culture that has
subjected him to a life of bitter hardship.

When Cambridge takes a stand to defend his slave-wife's honor,
he seals his own fate. And, in fact, his journal entries are made in des-
peration only days before he is to be hanged.

While in confinement, Cambridge writes: "It is man's duty . . . to
outwit tyranny in whatever form it appears." Such thoughts, derived
from his religious education in England, are all the more ironic since
Christian men of the motherland are about to take his life. He is holding their principles higher than they, presumably, ever imagined doing.

What does Caryl Philips mean to suggest by contrasting these two
characters? As he has in other works of fiction and nonfiction, Phillips
is interested in showing us the underbelly of colonialism, its original
conflicts, and the paradoxical origin of the black presence in the West.

In his 1987 essay collection, *The European Tribe,* Phillips concludes
that Europeans—especially Britons—must perform at least a private
"historical striptease" in order to purge themselves of their crimes
against Africa and the rest of the Third World and get on healthily with
their lives. The European tribe's more or less secure collective identity
has been achieved at a high price. "My presence in Europe is part of
that price," Phillips says. "I was raised in Europe [he was born in St.
Kitts in 1958, the same year that his parents emigrated to England] but
as I walked the tiny streets of Venice . . . I felt nothing . . . nothing inside
me stirred to make me rejoice" [yet] "we, black people, are an inextricable part of this small continent."

These reflections on the paradox of being in, but not of, Europe,
refer directly to the heart of Caryl Phillips's previous three novels, *The*

Final Passage (1985), *A State of Independence* (1986), and *Higher Ground* (1989). The two earlier novels are beautifully written and focus on unforgettable St. Kitts characters. In *The Final Passage* Phillips explores the factors that lead a young woman to pull up her roots from the British island colony of her birth and emigrate to England. Some readers might conclude that, on the evidence, it is not possible to completely leave home. Conversely, in *A State of Independence* Phillips follows the emotional and psychological journey of a St. Kitts native's return from England and his discovery that perhaps it is not possible to go home again.

That resolved or unresolved paradox is there in both novels. And there is a further subtext that speaks to the legacy of colonialism—the lives we enter are those of people born to its lingering effects. But Phillips's approach is not sociological, nor is his primary theme anything less than the human condition itself.

A NOVEL OF CONSEQUENCE

The Old Gringo, by Carlos Fuentes, Farrar, Straus & Giroux, 1985

At the time—1913—the novel *The Old Gringo* opens, Mexico is in a state of revolution. It is a "land of unconquered Indians and renegade Spanish, bold cattle rustlers and mines abandoned to the dark floods of hell."

Antagonism between the United States and Mexico is thick, General Pershing is poised, ready to go after Pancho Villa if Villa makes the wrong move; but the reader knows that Villa "could be killed only by the traitor within." Meanwhile, the real focus of Carlos Fuentes's story is on one of Villa's generals, Thomas Arroyo.

General Arroyo's sense of the United States is a place "... foreign and distant and curious, eccentric, marginal. . . . Yankees . . . did not enjoy good food or violent revolution or women in bondage." They "... broke with all tradition just for the sake of it, as if there were good things only in the future and in novelty. . . ."

The relationship between the two countries is important here only because two Americans—an old man (based on famed journalist Ambrose Bierce) called simply "the old gringo," and a woman school-teacher, Harriet Winslow—have just joined Arroyo's group of Villa supporters and fighters. Without their presence the story might be almost solely about the internal affairs of Mexico itself and the personal successes and failures of a few members of the brigade. In fact, in some ways the old gringo's and Miss Harriet's arrival on the scene seems forced; they sometimes seem to be there only to discuss the relations between the two countries.

But not always; they serve other ends as well.

The old gringo is seventy-two and has come to Chihuahua on his way to join Villa. He is ready to die, and wants to die in glorious battle. For the old muckraker, crossing the border (referred to at one point as a "scar") is symbolic; it is yet another frontier for a man who has run out of frontiers. He tells Arroyo that the unsafest frontier of all is "the frontier of our differences with others, of our battles with ourselves."

Miss Harriet, thirty-two, has come all the way from Washington, D.C., hired by mail as an English teacher for the children of the Mirandas, wealthy landowners. Since the Mirandas have been either killed or driven off by Villa's men by the time she arrives, she finds herself without an employer. On the spot she decides to stay anyway and teach English to the children of the brigade.

Miss Harriet has at least one thing in common with the old gringo: they both hate their fathers, and both their fathers are dead. She seeks a self-determined life, a way of being which was denied her back home, especially before her father went off to fight in the Cuban war and remained to spend the rest of his life living with a black woman.

In a sense, the old gringo too is here to fight not only for Villa but to continue his battle against his own dead father, whose powerful presence even in death still haunts him. When he rides alongside Arroyo into battle, he shoots toward the sky at "the father in the sky, a horseman of the sky, mounted forever on a Calvinist pulpit."

Other key members of the brigade are Mansalvo, La Garduna, and La Luna. Near the end, when Mansalvo is escorting Miss Harriet back to the border with the body of the old gringo, he laments that she hadn't become his lover. La Garduna is an old prostitute who travels with the fighters, apparently to service them. La Luna is Arroyo's mistress, a woman of remarkable humility and compassion who, as one might expect, tolerates Arroyo's misadventure with the American woman. In fact, she rejoices in it because of the pleasure it seems to bring him.

The Old Gringo succeeds more often than not. It is a serious book deserving serious attention.

NEW WORLD SCHEHERAZADE

The Stories of Eva Luna, by Isabel Allende, translated
from the Spanish by Margaret Sayers Peden, Atheneum, 1991

Rolf Carle, in the prologue to *The Stories of Eva Luna,* says to his
love, Eva Luna, "Tell me a story that you have never told to anyone before. Make it up for me." And she does it so well we forget that
the skillful fabulist Isabel Allende is her ventriloquist.

Some of the stories are told in the third person and others in the
first. Always complex and balanced with a blend of the supernatural
and what passes for reality, they explore the private and the public are-
nas of human affairs with equal devotion. Mystical and plush, the stories are usually both tragic and comic. They employ a diversity of
characters all too familiar to be exotic. If you like, call what Allende
does magic realism.

"Two Words" and "Wicked Girl" are good examples of Allende's
third-person form. In "Two Words," the first of the twenty-three stories, a young peasant woman, Belisa Crepusculario, hires a priest to
teach her to read and write, then sets out across her "inhospitable
land," presenting herself in village after village as a word merchant. For
five centavos, Belisa writes love letters, recites poems, or invents
insults. In short, she puts words in people's mouths for a reasonable
price. As a bonus, she also gives each of her customers a word that
becomes their own secret word, never to be shared with anybody else.

The Colonel, a rebel fighter in the hills—whose ambition is to
become president of this unnamed country—has her kidnapped and
brought to his encampment. She is commanded to write a campaign
speech that will ensure his victory. As she reads it to him, he memo-
rizes it, and when he recites the speech his voice sounds "as soft and
well-modulated as a professor's."

Physically attracted to the Colonel, "the loneliest man in the world," Belisa gives him a bonus of two secret words. Armed with her speech, he later wins the hearts of the people, but it is these two secret words she has planted in his soul that befuddle him and lead to the ending that I will not reveal here.

"Two Words" demonstrates Allende's fascination with complex combinations of the symbolic and the mystical. Belisa, a poor, powerless girl, herself becomes an ironic symbol of power, through her restless and enchanting use of language. The Colonel's childlike mystical faith in Belisa's ability leads him, ironically, to a destiny more complex than he bargained for.

Elena Mejías, the eleven-year-old protagonist of "Wicked Girl," is the daughter of a woman who runs a boardinghouse. One of Elena's jobs is to spy on the guests.

The arrival of one guest, Juan José Bernal, has a strange effect on the girl when she realizes her mother has become Bernal's mistress. Elena herself becomes obsessed by an erotic force linking her to the spirit of her mother's and Bernal's relationship.

Knowing that Bernal will be taking his afternoon nap, one day Elena sneaks into his room, strips, and manages to climb in bed beside him without waking him. Half awake, thinking the girl is his mistress, Bernal begins to make love to her. When he emerges completely from the fuzzy zone of half-sleep, his reaction is violent: He knocks the girl to the floor.

But the incident remains a secret as the story leaps far into the future. Elena and Bernal are in their separate ways victims of this secret. When Elena is twenty-six, she returns to visit her mother and Bernal. During a brief moment when they are alone, he confesses to having suffered years of guilt for having rejected her. When he begs for forgiveness, he learns something about her that is totally unexpected.

But let me simply say that the outcome is an example of the kind of irony and ambiguity that distinguish Allende's stories. Secrets, both suppressed and expressed, sometimes link people or generations. Sometimes the same secrets serve to break such human ties.

Irony, again, is at the crux of "And of Clay Are We Created," a richly textured first-person narrative told by Eva Luna about Rolf Carle as she observes him on a television screen. Rolf, a reporter, is covering the after-effects of an earthquake—"Twenty-thousand human beings and an indefinite number of animals putrefying in a viscous soup."

Allende's plot is mesmerizing. For three days and two nights, Rolf tries to dislodge Azucena, a thirteen-year-old girl, from a mud pit, all the while begging officials for a simple water pump to help free the girl. She is held down "by the bodies of her brothers and sisters clinging to her legs." Allende's ability to create and to sustain suspense is eloquently on display in this story. As engrossed as Eva Luna herself, we hold our breath in anticipation.

While waiting for a pump that nobody has made any effort to bring, Rolf and the girl talk, and the girl ironically manages to give him more comfort than he gives her, as he finds himself grief-stricken and vulnerable: "The girl had touched a part of him that he himself had no access to, a part he had never shared with me," Eva says. "Rolf had wanted to console her, but it was Azucena who had given him consolation."

As Azucena is dying, Rolf assures her that he loves her more than he has ever loved anyone. Hearing him say this to the girl, as she watches the television screen, Eva knows in her bosom that she would give anything to be in the dying girl's place.

But that is not the end of the story. The remarkable thing about this story—and Allende's fiction in general—is its refusal to channel the reader in a single emotional direction.

Allende's forte is irony and ambiguity, both usually rendered with wonderful subtlety. Allegories of human pain and strength, all the stories here are written with restraint and grace and, because they enchant like fairy tales, they recall the narrative force of ancient storytelling.

MAGICAL MYSTERY TOUR

Landscape Painted with Tea, by Milorad Pavic, translated from the
Serbo-Croatian by Christina Pribicevic-Zoric, Knopf, 1990

Most American readers and publishers of serious fiction seem more
willing to accept—and at times are even fascinated by—what we
loosely call experimental fiction as long as it comes from Europe or
South America. It can be dense, difficult, even boring, and such readers
still love it—love it as long as it is not written by an American writer.

This acceptance or infatuation is not unrelated to the fact that we
are enchanted by things foreign in general—accents, art, fashion. The
domestic intolerance for native experiments in fiction-making is
symptomatic of our historical and cultural inferiority complex. But
that is a subject for another occasion.

The example of an imported experimental novel at hand is
Yugoslav writer Milorad Pavic's *Landscape Painted with Tea.* A hugely
ambitious, playful, inventive, demanding, magical, and linguistically
sensuous reading experience, it is also hugely digressive and therefore
sometimes a swamp bed.

Pavic's model for the book's structure is supposed to be the crossword puzzle, with its down and across system. There are "down" tes-
timonials by the protagonist, Atanas Svilar / Atanas Fydorovich Razin,
a civil engineer, in which we see him ascend from poverty to unbe-
lievable wealth and keep notebooks in which he records his thoughts,
stories, observations, plans, and drawings.

The reading down idea—which takes place in time rather than in
the space on the page—also records the life of his second wife, Vitacha
Milut, who leaves her husband, Major Pohvalich, and their three
daughters in Belgrade and runs off to Vienna, and later to America,
with Atanas. Theirs is a tragicomic love story.

But "down" gives us much more—the life stories of three sisters, Cecilia, Arza, and Olga; Atanas's stories of trips abroad; relevant stories told by various other characters such as Atanas's mother, who later comes to fear her monstrously rich son.

Reading down, from Pavic's point of view, is the new way of reading. Reading "across" is the old (linear) way.

The "across" sections give us the old familiar but, in Pavic's hands, what is intended to be the unfamiliar as well. In the "across" scheme the narrator sets up a boobytrap network of compromises for the traditionalist. For those who like disorder there is disorder, for those who like order there appears to be order.

But this order is relative and limited. Numbered chapters, for example, are presented for lovers of order, but there's a catch: they are not in numerical order, a device echoing Steve Katz's 1972 novel *Saw*. Pavic's narrator says, "not everybody likes to read in order."

But most readers, the narrator seems to know, look for order— or, to use his expression, "well-arranged crossings." "What is a book, really, other than a collection of words well-crossed?" he asks. Pavic himself as author clings to order while professing the creative explosion of disorder.

One of Pavic's goals is to reorganize our experience of reading fiction (much as the late Donald Barthelme often did) so that we can see the familiar with fresh eyes. "Why . . . must the reader always be like a police inspector. . . . Why not let him at least zigzag somewhere?"

Once involved with *Landscape Painted with Tea,* the reader will indeed zigzag from beginning to end. In its big, sprawling way, it will take the reader through a staggering maze of thought and action— World War II, Catholicism, atheism, Satan, the Universe, death, Greek poetry, Byzantine liturgical song, Tito's various homes, cities such as Istanbul, Belgrade, Vienna, and huge chunks of the secular and sacred histories of Salonika, Syria, Mesopotamia, Egypt. These mental excursions amount to meditations.

Among many others in this linguistic, ideological, and philosophical scene-crossed text are reflections on Mount Athos and its two monastic lifestyles (the Cenobites and the Solitaries), the Danube, the Odyssey, the Adriatic Sea, astrology, and the nature of dreams.

Both the "down" and "across" sections are composed of long and short episodes. The short episodes—and the book is essentially a collection of them—tend to end with a surprising twist. The episodes with longer threads, those lasting to the end, follow the same principle. The reader will find that each twist reveals a moral. In this sense Pavic retains the spell of the old-fashioned storyteller.

But most of what Pavic wants the reader to reflect on comes not from Atanas himself but from those interesting minor characters, such as the ex-husband of his second wife, who comments on one of the obsessions of the book itself when he says:

> "What is the present? Our present is really the stoppage of time . . . this 'now' is the only common denominator of all living things. It is the only moment of life, from the beginning to the end of time, because everything else, the two eternities that stretch out before and after our 'now,' are in the deepest torpor. Consequently, the present is that part of the time which has stopped.

On another occasion a monk speaks: "A book, if you expect wonders of it, should . . . be read twice. It should be read once in youth, when you are younger than its heroes, and the second time when you are advanced in age and the book's heroes become younger than yourself. That way you will see them from both sides of their years, and they will be able to put you to the test on the other side of the clock, where time stands still. This means that it is forever too late to read some books, just as sometimes it is forever too late to go to bed. . . ."

I will not give away the ending of *Landscape Painted with Tea*. But I will say that it offers an "index," which is not to be read in the conventional way, and it leaves a lined space for the reader to write his or her own denouement.

In keeping with the business of a crossword puzzle, it also offers an upside-down "Solution." Several times throughout the novel, the narrator urges the impatient reader to quickly turn to these sections. My advice is not to take him seriously. The process of reading this novel—and novels like it—is what so-called experimental fiction is all about.

Aside from the idea of the crossword puzzle as a model for a novel, much of what may pass for technical innovation in Pavic's book

has already been done many times by such writers as Herman
Melville, Mark Twain, Gertrude Stein, Jean Toomer, Kenneth Patchen,
William Carlos Williams, and more recently John Barth, Donald
Barthelme, Ronald Sukenick, Robert Coover, and Russell Banks—to
mention only a few American writers.

In other words, Milorad Pavic, being hailed in Europe and
America as a groundbreaking writer, is merely joining an already illus-
trious international group without bringing to it much that is new.

AN IMPROBABLE LOVE
Cape of Storms: The First Life of Adamastor
by André Brink, Simon & Schuster, 1993

In André Brink's novella, *Cape of Storms,* one day near the end of the sixteenth century, a young white woman is left on a South African coastal beach by sailors, probably Portuguese, who had to make a hasty getaway after cheating and offending a nomadic tribe temporarily stopped near the beach. Why the woman was left and why she was on the ship in the first place, we never find out.

But really, it doesn't matter. What does matter is that the young tribal chief, T'kama, falls in love with this "bird" from the sea and she with him—that is, once she overcomes her fear of this strange place and these strange people with customs she doesn't understand. The chief and his tribe quickly depart, taking the woman with them. Trusting their god, Tsui-Goab, they follow rain and sun as they cross the desert in search of unspoiled places.

What evolves as they travel is a frustrated love story. Brink has given us a fable of an improbable love that takes long to consummate because of a big, big difficulty. But more about that later.

What's really refreshing is that the story can be read in several different ways. I think it would be a mistake simply to read it as a narrative of the historical roots of black-white conflict at the heart of South Africa's present-day racial nightmare. It's much more than the story of the first white men to drift onto the shores of South Africa, more than an interracial romance, or an attempt on the part of the white men to kill a black man over a white woman.

In a brief introduction, Brink talks about the Greek mythic models he had in mind for the book. Predictably, he meant T'kama to represent wildness, the untamed. By this I take Brink to mean he's trying

to get at the unrestrained creative powers of nature as represented by
these tribal people, and the way they live in rhythm with the weather
and the land. Though Eurocentric in perspective—despite being told
from the point of view of the tribal chief T'kama himself—this is not
another *Heart of Darkness*.

Kols—the name T'kama gives the white woman—is based on
the Greek sea-goddess Thetis, one of the Nereids, daughter of
Proteus and mother of Achilles. Thetis then must represent the sea,
and by extension, life. Not much in the story leads me to think she's
meant to represent that embattled, greed-driven process called "civilization" taking place at that time in Portugal—and the rest of
Europe for that matter.

Actually, Kols may represent some of the significance of her
father's relationship with Africa. Proteus, old man of the sea, is based
on an island off the Nile delta. In any case, his daughter, the "Nymph
and Princess of the Wave" (as represented by Kols), now land-bound,
adjusts quickly to tribal life, where she spends much of her time with
the other women and children, and even tries to be a good wife,
despite her homesickness.

But the big problem T'kama has to deal with is his penis. It's literally too big for Kols. And every time he thinks of consummating his
relationship with her, it gets bigger. At least in terms of his anatomy,
we're dealing with gigantism. T'kama is a sort of comic giant in a
reflexive text with chapter headings such as "A short chapter that may
be skipped by readers who object to descriptions of sexual intercourse."

As the tribe wanders the desert, thirsty and hungry, T'kama seeks
a solution to his problem. The wise elder of the tribe, Khamab,
believes that the luck of the tribe will change once T'kama is able to
mate with his strange wife.

Related in some ways to the tradition of the bawdy tale, *Cape of
Storms* even has a moment of cuckoldry. In their wanderings, they
come upon a tribe whose witch doctor vows to help T'kama. But the
herbal solution with which he treats the problem only makes it bigger and causes a terrible burning. While T'kama weeps in pain the
witch doctor seduces or attempts to seduce Kols. T'kama's penis now
grows so long he has to wrap it around his body several times to keep
it from dragging on the ground.

While, on the surface, this is comic and tragic, there is a profoundly relevant subtext. T'kama's problem is not simply a cruel trick
nature has played to conspire against the relationship. In fact, his problem might be read as no problem at all. He can be seen as a fertility
trickster figure, a kind of malevolent spirit.

Such a character requires a suspension of disbelief similar to the
kind needed to believe in Swift's little people, the Lilliputians, or
Voltaire's Micromegas, or the Cyclops of the *Odyssey* or Rabelais's
Gargantua, who starts out a giant and ends up a normal-size man. In
ancient tribal myths fertility demons such as these abound. The ancient
aboriginal people of Northeast Australia, for example, believed in fertility demigods, called Quinkans, who were blessed with penises so long
they could use them to pole-vault for great distances across the land.

In T'kama's case, a crisis proves a paradoxical solution of sorts.
Crazed with thirst, the tribe comes upon a river. Kols, the only one of
the group who can swim, jumps in and is immediately chased by a
crocodile. T'kama unwinds his penis and throws it like a rope to her
rescue; she pulls herself to safety.

Without giving away too much of the outcome, I can say that this
is a story for anyone who enjoys reading about troubled love or the
classic plights of fabled giants.

And it's funny.

THE UNBEARABLE WHITENESS OF BEING

Because It Is Bitter, and Because It Is My Heart
by Joyce Carol Oates, Dutton, 1990

Joyce Carol Oates's novel can be read as the story of a damsel in distress, who, after many trials and tribulations, comes through victoriously.

Oates's protagonist, Iris Courtney, might be a poor and unhappy Cinderella. Iris—with no special visionary inner light—by chance finds her way out of the nightmare of the unpromising circumstances of her birth into the comfort of a life of gentility and intellectual refinement. The emotional scars of her past and the fact that she does not feel comfortable in the role she has accepted is where the book ends.

Oates believes, as did James Baldwin, that the writer is here to bear witness. Although she does not resort to didacticism, the social and moral issues of her characters' lives are of paramount importance to her. One significant concept that emerges from Oates's investigation of these factors is the American invention of whiteness as a social norm. The concept emerges in contrast to the otherness of blackness.

Because It Is Bitter, and Because It Is My Heart (the title comes from a Stephen Crane poem) brings into focus not so much a love relationship between a white woman and a black man, but the wall of historical and social forces that prevent such a relationship from gaining momentum and moving toward a natural consummation.

The story is large and sprawling as it follows the loves of many characters in a small upstate New York town called Hammon, in the late 1950s and early sixties. But it is essentially the story of Iris Courtney, a troubled white girl with self-destructive parents whose lives reflect the general harshness of the town.

When Iris is menaced by Little Red Garlock, a white boy who is an obscene bully, she runs for help to Jinx Fairchild, a black basketball star at her high school. As Iris looks on, Jinx kills Red in self-defense. Thereafter, she and Jinx, in their separate ways, struggle with guilt and arrive, finally, at a bitter truce with themselves and the event.

As the years pass, Jinx attempts to avoid Iris, but Iris feels bonded to him for life. She finally tells her uncle—the only member of the family she respects—that she "loved" Jinx. This love for a black man—and her obsession with blackness—is at the center of the private, emotional life she cannot dislodge as she dispassionately enters respectable white upper-class society.

Images of herself magnified in whiteness as a sexual object crowd and flutter constantly in her mind. Grimly seeking release on the day President John F. Kennedy is shot, she goes, like a sleepwalker, into a black neighborhood, determined to find some sort of violent redemption to her obsession. She is kidnapped and beaten but not raped.

Soon after, the book closes with scenes of her preparing for marriage to the shallow son of the college professor she works for, who has all but adopted her.

In one sense, the novel is about the effects of the sexual tension underlying the exchange and conflict between black and white Americans. Although it advances no thesis, its events suggest that the antagonistic social and political forces that destroyed hope for Jinx are the same that shaped Iris's obsessive sexual fantasies. She even believes her future husband is turned on by the fact that black men have handled her white flesh.

Oates is a writer whose philosophical questing, as expressed here and in many of her novels, frequently ends with inconclusive, provisional summations. This tendency leads to anti-conclusions, which are more satisfying than the tight and terrible discomfort of the dogmatic, single vision of life.

This book's style is lyrical and impressionistic at its best and choppy at its worst. Full of broken thoughts and images, it is a tapestry of bits and pieces that, in the end, add up impressively to a whole—if awkward—and wondrous thing.

The narrative voice itself operates at a considerable distance from the action, sustaining the effect that the implied author is unquestionably in control. Occasionally the voice is annoying because of its teacherly evaluations of human behavior. But the payoff is that the reader is not allowed to get caught up sentimentally in the emotional life of the characters. Although this may disappoint those seeking escape into action and romance, it is a quality that will continue to endear Oates to readers who find pleasure in the greater challenge of a self-apparent text.

REFLECTIONS ON A NATIVE SON

James Baldwin: The Legacy, edited by Quincy Troupe,
Simon & Schuster, 1989

James Baldwin: Artist on Fire, by W. J. Weatherby,
Donald I. Fine, Inc., 1989

In thinking about James Baldwin's contribution to American culture, there is much that remains unclear. What does at the moment seem apparent is that his career was both astonishing and sadly disappointing. He once said to me, "Success is as difficult to handle as failure," and I had the feeling that he had dwelled in both places all his life.

James Baldwin wanted more than anything, I think, to be a great novelist. He believed firmly in his ability to write fiction and he beamed like an innocent child when he was complimented. But was he a great novelist, or even a good one? I grew up on his novels and recently reread most of them. What I found there was passion but too much sentimentality, a distinct literary style but too much that was mannered and clichéd. I have no idea how history will read James Baldwin, but for me, right now, his greatness does not reside in the body of fiction he left us.

Baldwin's strength was in his profound understanding of the human condition and in his equally profound understanding of human history. He knew where we came from, so to speak, and that was why he was so good at telling us where we were. Although he tried to do this in his novels, he did it better in his essays. These essays have, of course, always been celebrated for their brilliant insights into the issues of race, but Baldwin was never simply talking about black-white matters. His subject was the human condition.

A dozen books about the life and works of James Baldwin appeared during his lifetime. Dozens more are bound to appear now that he is dead and his work complete. The two under review here differ greatly in their objectives, but both have their uses. Troupe's collection makes no claim to being definitive. It is a gallery of eighteen pieces—articles and speeches and interviews—divided into five sections, the last one containing reprints of Baldwin's famous essay, "Notes of a Native Son," and his introduction to the overlooked but important collection, *The Price of the Ticket* (1985). (I perhaps unfairly wished that Troupe had added one of the most important and deeply personal essays Baldwin wrote, "Here Be Dragons," which appears at the end of that collection.)

But Troupe's own introduction and his interview with Baldwin just before he died, as well as Chinua Achebe's article, are enough to make the book worth the price. These are deeply personal and moving documents. In reading them I could see and hear the Jimmy I knew. The memorial speeches by Imamu Amiri Baraka, Toni Morrison, and Maya Angelou delivered at the funeral at St. John the Divine and the appreciation by Mary McCarthy are also here. They echo the aesthetic and political sentiments one normally associates with these writers. Baraka seems ambivalent toward Baldwin, Morrison and Angelou compassionate and loving. McCarthy? Perhaps both charmed and fearful of this "elegant," erratic, heavy-drinking black man she had known since the 1940s.

There is no point in wondering why these pieces, old and new, were selected from the thousands available. In all probability they were the ones within reach. When many conflicting views of a human being and his work exist and the anthologist wants to extract a coherent impression, the task is not light. When one's subject has many faces from which to choose—political activist, novelist, poet, essayist, public personality—it is even harder. Troupe's book leaves the impression of a personal scrapbook, which is probably all it should be.

Weatherby's effort is far more ambitious. This unauthorized biography is important because it takes some first brave steps toward reporting Baldwin's life and trying to relate it to his work. Weatherby seems to understand that what was important about James Baldwin was his consciousness, his presence as a social witness.

The book consists of twenty-two chapters. In them Weatherby shows us the stages of Baldwin's life from its beginning in Harlem to his funeral procession that wound its way through the same neighborhood, bringing his life, as Weatherby says in an easy metaphorical connection, full circle.

Baldwin's early shyness, his anxiety over and obsession with the mystery of who his real father was, his feelings of being ugly ("Frog Eyes"), his encounters with racism during the war when he worked on the railroad, the loss of a friend to suicide, his early bohemian life, the rejection of his first novel, are explored with impressive journalistic skill.

Although none of this information is new, Weatherby weaves it all together in a way that suggests the sprawling, intensely chaotic, and driven nature of Baldwin's life. Measured against the polished and highly focused nature of his best work it is easy to understand why diamonds are formed in the earth at the point of the most intense pressure.

Weatherby's descriptions of Baldwin's early life in Paris (based largely on fresh interviews with other members of that bohemian American colony) add something to Baldwin's own well-known essays about his early years in Paris in the forties: Down and out, he often found himself among *"les miserables"*—the Algerians—living on handouts. Baldwin was one of the first Afro-American novelists to carry out a literary investigation of the French-Arab exchange and conflict in France. I refer to such essays as "Equal in Paris" and stories like "This Morning, This Evening, So Soon." In doing so he followed the example set by another Afro-American novelist, William Gardner Smith, who lived most of his adult life in Paris and explored the subject in his novel from the early 1960s, *The Stone Face.*

If Weatherby tries to use a unifying theme to hold the book together—and that's a hard claim to make—it is Baldwin's anguish over the circumstances of his birth, an anguish directly related to the high price James Baldwin had to pay to "keep [his] own heart free of hatred and despair." Perhaps a more suitable theme might have been the essential ingredients of Baldwin's consciousness that made him a witness to the human heart in the modern world.

A SICKNESS OF THE SOUL

Fever: Twelve Stories, by John Edgar Wideman, Holt, 1989

Suffering and the quest for redemption are what most of the stories in John Edgar Wideman's second collection, *Fever,* are about.

The word "fever" becomes a metaphor for both suffering and injustice. The nineteenth-century black doctor treating Philadelphia yellow fever victims in the title story rejects explanations that the fever comes from ships fleeing insurrection in Santo Domingo. "To explain the fever we need no boatloads of refugees, ragged and wracked with killing fevers, bringing death to our shores," he muses. "We have bred the affliction within our breasts. . . . Fever grows in the secret places of our hearts, planted there when one of us decided to sell one of us to another."

Although the other eleven stories are set in the present century, in one way or another they echo the sentiment of the fever metaphor. The legacy of slavery is the common denominator. But Wideman's characters, white and black, exist with irony in the stage setting of this history.

An example of this irony plays around the question of vision as enlightenment, which becomes a form of redemption in Wideman's hands. In "When It's Time to Go," Sambo, a blind piano player, concludes that what is important about humanity—despite suffering and callousness—is its continuation.

Another blind character, the narrator of "Doc's Story," recovers from a broken heart when he is transformed by the courage and faith of a blind basketball player.

Broken hearts come in various forms in Wideman's stories but so does the questing for recovery. An elderly Jew, whose life was saved by a black woman in a prison camp during the war, attempts to make sense of his own luck and life through an effort to communicate with the black woman who has cleaned for him for decades. A black intellectual struggles to understand the hostage crisis and the Middle Eastern conflict between the Jews and the Arabs. In the process he discovers there are many unfortunate ways in which people hold each other hostage. And the captive is always a victim of violence.

This threat of violence links the stories as much as does the theme of suffering and redemption. A quiet violence, for example, permeates "The Statue of Liberty." The narrator, who is white, invites a black jogger (and his white female companion) into her home for "cool drinks." When she has herself and them naked in chairs arranged in a V with the man at the base, the violence of her erotic fantasies erupts, leaving the mysterious—almost terrifying—presence of the ghost of all human desire.

But ghosts and lost souls are everywhere in these stories. In "Rock River," the ghost is the blood left on the seat of a truck where a man has been killed. The blind man of "When It's Time to Go" lives constantly with the magical presence of his own ghost. Fever, in the title story, makes its ghostly presence felt through "vomiting and diarrhea, helplessness, delirium," and "convulsions."

Lest I be misunderstood, this is not a pessimistic book. Even so, the reader earns an uneasy truce with the writer because any particular moral conclusion must be tempered with a final uncertainty, except over the issues of cruelty and injustice. Because the characters are so complex and richly textured, the situations rendered with such an even hand, the reader's sympathies are not one-sided.

Stylistically, the stories are impressionistic, with pointillistic touches. The constantly shifting points-of-view give them a cubist touch as well. Wideman's narrative voices have strong, clear personalities. But his prose is always, more or less, the hero of his fiction. He avoids closure, to characters as well as to stories. Who, then, are his literary ancestors? I would say he loves or once loved Sterne, Joyce, and Faulkner.

As with almost any collection, some of the stories are better than others. "Fever" itself is the most ambitious while "Valaida," "The Statue of Liberty," and "Hostages" seem the most artistically successful.

The weaker ones gain, though, by association with the stronger. "Little Brother," a warm-hearted, nostalgic, sentimental fiction about a dog; "The Tambourine Lady," about a smart girl's world of the familiar comforts of home and church; "Presents," about a boy whose grandmother represents his means to understanding, compassion, and reverence, gain much for coming after more profound stories such as "Valaida," "Hostages," and "When It's Time to Go." "Fever," at the end, is a deep historical echo, coming up from the belly of time, the way "Kabnis" does at the end of Jean Toomer's *Cane* (1923).

Even "Surfiction"—the least satisfying story here—does not seem too far out of place although I am convinced that it is possible to read it as an essay without the slightest bit of trouble.

There has always been a kind of thematic and stylistic ambivalence in John Wideman's work. It is hard to say precisely what it is all about, but my guess would be that he is constantly torn between a commitment to representational writing and all the other kinds of technical innovations he tries. In total, this conflict comes out as positive and correlates with the sense of moral and cultural paradox through which his characters are created.

AN ALPHABET OF FUTURE NIGHTMARES

Zulus, by Percival Everett, The Permanent Press, 1990

Primarily because of his remarkable first novel, *Suder* (1983), Percival Everett is considered by a growing number of readers of serious contemporary fiction to be one of America's most promising younger novelists. *Zulus,* his speculative and much more ambitious fourth novel, adds to that promise.

Purely in terms of subject matter I was reminded of Huxley's *Brave New World* and Orwell's *1984.* There are also thematic parallels to Margaret Atwood's *The Handmaid's Tale.*

In *Zulus* the reader is dropped into a post-thermonuclear future that alternates between looking suspiciously like the present and like the Dark Ages. It is a nightmare in which our worst fears come true without ever truly terrifying us because the events remain unreal.

The two main settings are the nameless city and the countryside. The city-dwellers are zombies. The women are sterilized at an early age and the human race is dying. The people have little more than cheese to eat. Fruit is difficult to find.

The protagonist of this strangely unreal novel is a grossly fat woman named Alice Achitophel. Due to an oversight she has not been sterilized, so when she is raped by a drifter she becomes pregnant. This fact makes her of great interest to rebels who want to regenerate the human race. After being captured and escaping from the rebels—liberated from her fat by an act of the imagination—Alice meets her prince charming, Kevin Peters, and hope for the human race seems to glow for a second or two.

The best scenes are intentionally at once strange and familiar. They are slippery. They can give you the shivers. The would-be rapist arrives on Alice's front porch. His request is simple: May he stand here and watch the snow falling? Later Alice, with the band of rebels in the countryside, is sucked into the womblike muck of an embankment.

The paradoxical tension between the strange and the commonplace eventually dissolves completely. The scene of Alice's rebirth from fat to thin is a surrealistic Dali landscape of melting flesh and utero-vaginal fury. It is matched in imaginative intensity one other time in the book, near the end during a nightmare death and burial scene where, symbolically, the whole human race dies, presumably in order to be reborn.

But what is most interesting about *Zulus* is its display of the author's interest in language and its relation to the activity of the imagination. There are many isolated moments that are fascinating in purely aesthetic and cultural terms, especially in the brief italicized paragraphs that open each chapter. Here's one:

> G is for Ganymede whom Zeus carried, eagle-clad, far to the top
> of Olympus, taking him en route. A feather up his cap. G is for
> gluttony. G is for Garvey and Gabriel and some in Guyanna,
> keeping 'distance from the thickening center.' G is for 'Grab your
> ankles, America.' Receive the goods. The gift is a goose from God.
> God is for sodomy. G is for Goya, who knew.

In these sections, Everett's gifts as a lyrical writer are vividly on display. His ear for music in the alphabet of words reminds me of Ezra Pound's comment in *The ABC of Reading*: "Music rots when it gets *too far* from the dance. Poetry atrophies when it gets too far from music."

The echo of James Joyce—"Do tell us all about. As we want to hear allabout. So tellus tellas allabouter. . . ."—is also evident in Everett's narrative. Listen to this: "E is for Ellison and his optic white, sitting invisible on the outside edge of history, watching what can never be. E is for Earwicker. His will be done."

Zulus is a curious, troublesome, and, at times, delightful addition to the literature of the anti-heroic and the futuristic.

CLARK'S YORK

In Search of York, The Slave Who Went to the Pacific with Lewis and Clark
by Robert B. Betts, Colorado Associated University Press, 1985

President Thomas Jefferson wanted to know what was out there beyond the known frontier. In 1803, to find out, he commissioned Captain Meriwether Lewis to go as far west as he could, or till he came to the ocean that somehow had to be there. The story is well-known; however, the popularized version which has come down to us little resembles the report Lewis and Clark left in their journals or other contemporary evidence. A case in point: As they explored the vast reach of unmapped land from the midwest to the Pacific, Clark had, in addition to Lewis, the companionship of his slave and friend from childhood, York. There were a total of eleven men at the beginning of the expedition. Popular myth has it that York primarily provided comic relief for his ten companions.

Robert N. Betts's book, *In Search of York, The Slave Who Went to the Pacific with Lewis and Clark,* is a brave attempt to set the record straight about York. It is not surprising that York, a slave, and black, has been "a man history has passed by," or, more correctly, maligned. Betts brilliantly—and calmly—resurrects York (and he does it as well as anyone is likely to be able to at this late date) from the ashes of racist history-making.

Betts assures us that there is no evidence that York spent all his time screwing the Indian women along the way and encountered dozens of his offspring on the return trip, as the mythifiers would have it. "Nowhere," says Betts, "in any of the journals kept while the expedition was in progress is any reference made to him [York] and the Indian women." As it turns out, the only recorded reference (during York's lifetime) to his so-called sexual activity with Indian women was made by a couple of popular writers. As Betts notes, "The journals actually say less about him [York] with regards to members of the opposite sex than . . . about his white companions, a number of whom [unlike York] had to be treated for venereal disease. . . ." In addition, Betts could find no evidence to back up the ". . . sweeping assertions that he [York] was sought out and bedded down all along the expedition's route."

Since his time much slanderous writing about York in this vein has been passed off as scholarship or creative work. Among the better-known culprits Betts cites Vardis Fisher and Robert Penn Warren; among the lesser-known ones, Olin Wheeler and Elijah Criswell. Historians, novelists, and poets warped the image of York into ". . . a comic character [designed] to evoke laughter."

There is evidence that, for a few of the Indians, York was "big medicine." He was viewed (because of his apparent strength and Blackness) "with astonishment and awe." Example: the Shoshonis gave much-needed horses to Lewis and Clark because, and solely because, ". . . the black man . . . excited [their] curiosity." Without the horses, the group almost certainly would have had to turn back.

There were also, however, specific acts for which York was responsible that made his participation significant. Among the men with Lewis and Clark, York was one of the few who could swim (on a trip taken largely by rivers) and he spoke several Indian languages. York often "disregarded his own safety" to help his master and, apparently, the other men. His survival skills either matched or exceeded those of anyone among the crew. Not socially isolated on this particular trip because of his station in life, York was, in fact, the first known member of his race to cross the American West and, it now can be seen, clearly helped to make the crossing possible.

However, as might be expected, the story did not have a happy ending. York had grown up with Clark. As children they had played, fished, and hunted together. During the years of the expedition they were apparently still on friendly terms. Nevertheless, after the expedition, the relationship changed for some reason.

Betts tell us that the minute the trip ended, in 1806, all the explorers—except York—were celebrated by their countrymen. This, of course, is not surprising, given his status and the return to "civilization." But, ". . . perhaps as early as 1809, and almost surely no later than the spring of 1810, York was no longer a member of the Clark house-hold in St. Louis," Betts writes. Clark, according to a recently discov-ered letter, sent York to Louisville to be with his wife which also meant being leased to serve another plantation owner who physically abused York horribly. The letter also makes clear that York and Clark had had a serious "falling out" which caused York to fear he might never regain Clark's "good graces."

Thus, contrary to the popularized belief, Clark did not grant York freedom immediately after the expedition. True, Clark had already made lofty talk about the wrongness of slavery. His state of mind was clearly torn. But, in the end, York ". . . fell from the highly favored sta-tus of a body servant to one of the lowest of all slave positions, a hired-out slave." The same thing would happen to Frederick Douglass.

"We can see," finally, "a York much more complex than we have been conditioned to think, a York much more important to the suc-cess of the expedition than we have been told, and a York much more tragically a victim of slavery than we have been given to believe," con-cludes Betts. Unfortunately, the appearance of this much needed book will not change the myths about York. They are needed by the people who made them—and the true record is not.

JEROME CHARYN: INNOVATIVE DETECTIVE

Blue Eyes, Simon & Schuster, 1974

New York is a crowded place and as an extension of it, so is *Blue Eyes,* Jerome Charyn's eighth work of fiction.

The main character of *Blue Eyes* is Manfred "Shotgun" Coen. Coen, who eats animal crackers and American cheese, has lost his wife and kids to a dentist. Coen is a cop with beautiful cheeks and no respect for concepts. His parents killed themselves, primarily, because gentility cannot exist on Boston Road in the Bronx. The loss of a refined mother and a dignified father left Coen in the classic condition of "searching" for replacements. He found a father figure in Chief Isaac, who has Coen thinking he (the Chief) has been busted for taking payoffs from organized gamblers. (The Chief goes around in a beggar's outfit stinking to high heaven.) Coen, here, is doubly betrayed: Isaac fails both as father image and trusted friend.

Coen, who is good at stroking the egos of his superiors, still sees his wife, Stephanie, who is also a kind of maternal figure. Stephanie left Coen because of his obscene cop talk. He returns to her because ping-pong parlors are lonely places and chasing missing persons is no fun. Stephanie is not simply a "cunt" (though many of the minor female characters are seen as such, for instance by rookie cops).

Coen's neighbor, Mrs. Dalkey, the yenta, is also a "person," who has, like Coen, a devastated past. She, in fact, emerges in ways not available to Stephanie. Mrs. Dalkey captures Ernesto, the infamous lipstick freak, who is also the dog poisoner. Coen's real mother, like his real father, is two-dimensional, flat. They leave him a legacy of pain and despair. But the effect of this (and every other aspect of the book's content) is not emotional. This is because Charyn is concerned with something other than allowing the reader a chance to suffer or laugh.

Odile Lonhardy is the main female character. She is a nineteen-year-old prostitute, a porno queen who, by the time Coen dies, has "worn vaginal jelly for a hundred and five men," and has a dog named Valesquez. Valesquez chokes on a wishbone and dies. Odile (also called Odette) lights three candles for the animal but feels nothing when people die. Odile is clearly not a mother figure. Unlike Stephanie or Mrs. Dalkey, Odile is the classical erotic dream strumpet. It is not the real Odile that the Chinaman, Chino Reyes, Coen, and the cop, Pimlo, lust after, but their own vision of her.

Caroline Child is a shadow of a young woman. Fine. Rounded characters are out. In order to understand what Charyn intends one must remember that this is basically a literary potboiler, a whodunit, a detective story that, first of all, is concerned with its own thrust, its own plot. And Caroline (like other characters in various degrees) is simply a problem the reader is asked implicitly to solve. One does not, then, look for her (or any of them) to emerge.

Still, on a *content* level, we have Herbert Pimlo, the Harvard goy inspector; Isobel, the portorriquena switchboard operator with a weakness for cops; Emo "The Great" Baskin, a white Forty-second Street pimp; Uncle Sheb who needs only two dollars and toilet paper; Soloman Wong (Chino's father), a bindle stiff and dishwasher who sleeps in a garbage can; Spanish Arnold, the cripple stool pigeon; Jeronimo, "A subnormal who couldn't survive without a lump of caramel in his mouth" (p. 108); a bunch of tough lesbians who run the Dwarf, where Odile hangs out; Janice, a former handwrestling queen at the Women's House of Detention; Piss, a wino-ex-vaudevillian; and a bright parade of persons identified variously as a pacifist vegetarian Austrian Jew, chinks, spics, niggers, goms, rats, rookies, punks, jigs, shitheads, palookas, yids, bulls, geeks, bloodhounds, soulkissers, bagel babies, freaks, and superfreaks.

Coen and Chino are on bad terms from the beginning. They engage in a wrestling match at Cesar Guzmann's (one of the small-time thugs). So, when the final confrontation comes in a dingy ping-pong parlor run by Shiller, there is no surprise. The Chinaman shoots

Coen in the neck then the supercops (Defalco, Rosenheim, and Brown) rush in and shoot Chino to pieces.

Prior to the ping-pong parlor bloodshed, the reader sees Coen angrily warning Chino not to ever touch his (Coen's) daughters again. This is after they bring Caroline Child back from Mexico and before Coen has sex with Odile, an act Chino desperately seeks but never accomplishes.

Blue Eyes is filled with quick, vivid scenes, each a lyrical parody of naturalism. Witness: in a cab Odile kisses a wiped-out man. "Her tongue licked the flats of his teeth. Even the cabby was suspicious. He wouldn't believe such kissing could exist in his own cab." (p. 181) Coen plays ping-pong with Shiller: "Standing close to the table he took Shiller's balls right off the hop and fed them into the corners. . . ." (p. 117) The scene shifts briefly to Mexico where Coen and Chino track Caroline, who's being held in a "pink stucco on Darwin Street off Shakespeare." (p. 101) Soon, "Coen lifted the tails of his jacket to air his pistol butts." (p. 101)

But Coen is not a supercop and certainly not a superhero. When we see him with Uncle Sheb, with Steffie, Mrs. Dalkey, and with Vander Child (Caroline's father), we know him as a person (in a way) burdened with shortcomings.

But Coen is not (nor are others here) really the center of attention. It would be an oversimplification to say that this is a detective story concerned with Coen's successful delivery of Caroline Child to her father; or with Chief Isaac's undercover attempt to bust a ring of gangsters, headed by Papa Guzmann and his son, Cesar; or with the Chinaman's unsuccessful attempt to seduce Odile; or even with the isolation and loneliness of isolated and lonely people who are corrupt policemen or compassionate crooks. As layers of assumptions are peeled away we discover beneath the fabric of each relation the false impressions these characters hold about each other. So, in one sense, detection here is extended beyond the customary boundaries of the genre.

Charyn is primarily interested in exploiting and revitalizing the possibilities of the detective novel. The self consciousness of the technique, the explosively brilliant use of language, the comic undercurrents, the grotesque and commonplace characters brought together are serious signals of what Charyn is really up to.

Charyn's previous novels can also serve as a key to what he is attempting to do in *Blue Eyes*. Every bit as conventional as *Once Upon a Droshky* (1964), *Blue Eyes* lacks the imaginative thrust present in *Eisenhower, My Eisenhower* (1971). While it is more readable than *The Tar Baby* (1973)—Charyn's most ambitious and original novel—*Blue Eyes* is still not mass market fiction.

Blue Eyes is dense, with point of view deliberately diffused. It is decked with ethnic and vocational slang, bright with the cheap glitter of Lower Manhattan and the wilderness of the Bronx; stylistically, it both laughs at and honors Hemingway and Chandler. Though far more static than *On the Darkening Green* (1965) and *Going to Jerusalem* (1967), *Blue Eyes* can easily become Jerome Charyn's best-known book. That would not be a unique sort of irony.

SOMEWHERE OVER THE RAINBOW

Liliane: Resurrection of the Daughter
by Ntozake Shange, St. Martin's, 1994

Performance is the key word to understanding the work of poet Ntozake Shange. In 1976 when her play *for colored girls who have considered suicide / when the rainbow is enuf* opened on Broadway, her future as an artist with an ear for the music of language and the "combat breath" (Fanon) of political consciousness was secure.

Although she did not give up the stage as a place for working out the final performance version of her writing, much of her reputation later rested not on her staged performances, but on what she actually wrote and published as a poet and prose writer.

In her novel, *Liliane,* performance is everything. We learn by way of an acknowledgment note that the book was tested on the stage by performers. Little wonder the voices are pitch perfect to the ever-present music. And Shange makes the language of her culture dance to that music.

The protagonist, Liliane Lincoln, elusive, volatile, complex, and sophisticated, is presented to us, in part, through twelve vivid monologue performance pieces narrated in turn by her and her friends and lovers. Liliane's ideal world, as they present it, is a world in which all of her own and the world's "contraries" could exist in harmony. This world would be free of stereotypes, hypocrisy, racism, serious class differences, and destructive self-effacement.

Liliane crosses class, racial, and national lines, inventing her own language as she blazes her way toward this utopia. Her friends believe themselves blessed to have known her.

Liliane (or Lili) herself narrates only the first and fifth monologues. At the beginning she is (and she remains so till the end) a young woman with deep, unresolved family issues. This conflict is caused largely by the strife of her early years. These years were presided over by her domineering father, Judge Parnell Lincoln, who is something of a god in the family and community. Her mother, Sunday Bliss LaFontaine Lincoln, remains a secret, a mystery, a disgrace.

The action takes place all over the country and beyond. The Lincolns move from New Jersey to St. Louis and back. Liliane interacts with her assortment of friends and lovers in Queens, Manhattan, the San Francisco Bay Area, Mississippi, Texas, St. Louis, East St. Louis, Paris, France, and a few other places. Not in the least bound by geographical location, home is where Liliane happens to dig in her spurs.

Her best friends, Roxie, Lollie, and Bernadette, have been just that since childhood. Her lovers (the main ones) Thayer, Victor-Jesus, Sawyer, and Zoom, are themselves complex characters so different from each other that, by association with them, Liliane's already complex personality becomes even more complex and ultimately elusive.

While more questions are raised than are answered, the personalities of friends and lovers reveal more about themselves while "rapping" about Liliane than they reveal about her in her fragmented reality.

Despite her complexity, for her, falling in love is simple. She does it mostly at first sight. Something magical clicks with certain males and, bingo, she's in over her head.

But who are these "boyfriends" or main lovers and what do they mean to Liliane? Her first love: Sawyer Malveau III, "Creole," rich, spoiled, of the Talented Tenth (like herself), is shot dead before he is a man. Her white love: Joel (known as Zoom), rides a Harley and blows sax like Charlie Parker circa 1948. But this relationship too is doomed from the beginning because Liliane can't give her heart to a white guy no matter how cool he is. Her daddy would die. And she knows that one of these days she herself would explode and do something terrible to him. Then there is her Manhattan lover, Thayer, who tells us about her life as an artist in Manhattan. And the Frenchman, Jean-Rene, spotted in a Paris Greek fast-food joint eating souvlaki, wins her heart on the spot.

But none of these guys seem able to get a handle on Liliane. While in her teens, Granville Simeon, her date at a party, is violently confronted by Danny Stuyvesant, another one of her male devotees. With each lover or potential lover, something always goes wrong. Victor-

Jesus Maria (a Spanglish-speaking colored kid) who presents himself in the role of an ex-lover who protectively monitors Liliane's life of many skirmishes (and a few touchdowns), prevails at least as a friend.

From Liliane's point of view, men generally are too focused on sex, taking it far too seriously. She has to be careful not to laugh. But all she wants, really, is "a technologically proficient Third World man to enter the twenty-first century" with her. (p. 214) Fed up with failed relationships, she says: "I'm not going to come out of my house until there are some hip black people in outer space." (214)

And the girlfriends? One of the great sources of Liliane's grief is the loss of her best friend Roxie, killed by Roxie's boyfriend, Tony. Liliane has bad dreams about Roxie's daughter, Sierra. Hyacinthe (Saywer's sister) is like a sister to Liliane. She ends up—quite sane, by the way—in an insane asylum with Liliane's drawings all around the walls. "Hoodlum" cousin Lollie LaFontaine knows everything about Liliane. Bernadette, a New Jersey high school pal, also seems to know Liliane better than Liliane knows herself.

These glittering monologues are interspersed with twelve blocks of dramatic dialogue in which two voices are suspended in space against a kind of Beckettian emptiness. In fact the blocks of dialogue take place in a "Room in the Dark." In the intense exchange between Liliane and her analyst, angry and ranting, she sincerely tries to sort through the complexity and pain of her life.

She's trying to understand why her mother ran off with a white man, why her father lied to her about it, why her best friend, Roxie, was murdered, why America is so full of racism, why there is such a lack of vision in the world, and why there is so little respect for the little that is here, and why she herself has had such rotten luck with men.

The dramatic dialogues accent and comment upon the monologues. Although the reverse isn't the case, perhaps much of Liliane's agony anticipates, as a kind of subtext, their necessity. So, in this sense, subtle and overt thematic unity crisscross, matching the crossfire between her and her analyst.

Liliane is a spirited book with a wealth of convincing and true African American voices talking love and pain, survival and endurance. And they surround this richly complex woman, Liliane, in all her eccentricity and beauty, with their performances.

Much has been written both about performance and representation in the novel, as we know it, and the death of the novel as a literary form. *Liliane: Resurrection of the Daughter,* is Ntozake Shange's answer to the question, "Is there anything new to be done with the novel as performance?"

BOOKED SOLID

Extravaganza, by Gordon Lish, G.P. Putnam and Sons, 1989

Gordon Lish's novel, *Extravaganza,* is not dependent on linear progression. It proceeds by way of a sequence of discontinuous episodes. In these episodes he embraces three strategies: literary theory banter, vaudeville gags, and the murkier territory of the comedy of mortality and identity.

The second and most successful strategy is the string of episodes modeled on the classic skits of burlesque comedy, where two jokers come out on the stage to warm up the audience with a brief stint of low comedy, in other words, "dirty" jokes, before the main event (striptease acts) starts. Lish's specific model is the vaudeville team of Smith and Dale—both now deceased and "laid out side by side." The stone says: "Booked Solid."

The reason this aspect of the book seems to me to be the most successful has to do with its directness, humor, and honesty. For example, in one of these episodes Mrs. Smith makes her husband go downstairs to get a haircut from the new handsome young barber. Mr. Smith comes back and reports that the barber bragged about having seduced every woman in the building except one. Mrs. Smith responds by saying, "So what would you like to bet me it's that stuck-up doctor's wife up there on eleven?"

Many of his jokes are old and well-known and reshaped—but not much—by Lish: Mostly there are doctor and patient jokes. Smith goes to the doctor and Dale is always the doctor—"Are you the doctor? I am the doctor." Just as in the classic vaudeville skits, the patient is worried that he might have a heart problem or worms or something worse. But the doctor responds not with a cure but a wisecrack.

There are almost as many New York Jewish jokes. Example: In
response to anonymous violently obscene and anti-Semitic telephone
calls, Mrs. Smith says, "So you know all that from just hello?"

There's the one about the husband who comes home and finds his
wife in bed while cigar smoke is coming from the bedroom closet; the
one about the two brothers, the dead cat, and the dead mother.

But there are many other kinds of jokes: Jokes about what to buy
one's wife for an anniversary, about orgasm, eating disorders, proposi-
tioning a hooker, playing golf, acting, dealing with the tailor or the
travel agent, fishing for or eating herring for breakfast, riding the train,
dealing with the stationmaster, and even a retelling of "The Farmer in
the Dell."

The effect is often captivating for a reader who is familiar with
burlesque comedy and vaudeville. Seeing the skits done as fiction conjures up the essential spirit of not only Smith and Dale's act but the
whole theatrical tradition that produced George Burns, Sophie Tucker,
Jack Benny, Bob Hope, Redd Foxx, and many others. But perhaps the
concept of the book depends too heavily on a reader being aware of
that history. Truly great works of art achieve a stunning degree of independence, in terms of clarity and integrity, from outside reference.

The other clear strategy is a kind of banter between the two main
characters, Smith and Dale, on literary theory, humor, the importance
of riddles, maybe even life itself. Smith and Dale occasionally take
time out to discuss the process of their fun-making. At one point
Smith says to Dale: "We got to stop it with the wisecracks." He's being
absolutely ironic: Lish's characters have nothing new to add to the
already staggering body of imaginative theory on these subjects. But
that may be the point.

On the other hand, this whole strategy may be intended as a mock-
ery of "experimental" fiction writing as we know it in our time. Some
of its seems to echo or perhaps mock Samuel Beckett. But even more
to the point, Lish lashes out sweetly with "Pages, pages, pages . . . of paragraphs, of sentences, of words . . ." by way of Smith and Dale: "This is
just a book, Mr. Smith," and, "Thank God for the brilliant genius
which is knocking his brains out to sit himself down and think up this
beautiful book," and, ". . . lovely book, Mr. Smith," and, "Could a book
be off to a more wonderful start as a book, Mr. Dale?"

The murkier territory is represented by episodes that lend an odd depth to the book's otherwise lighthearted—I hesitate to say superficial—tone. They happen most often in the last part of the book in impressive leaps of the imagination as Lish tries to bring it all together as he moves toward its finish. Here, earlier events intermingle, challenge each other, dance the dance of refrain.

In these later parts, even the comedy becomes more sophisticated, especially as it is brought more sharply to the question of identity. Although from the beginning Smith and Dale play the comedy of mortality and identity—"Dr. Dale . . . my name is Smith, my name is not Feigenbaum"—that comedy does not transcend tiresome repetition and verbosity until the episodes are shorter and less slapstick for slapstick's sake.

In reading *Extravaganza* I had mixed reactions. On the plus side, the quality of the experience, especially in the last third of the book, nearly matched that considerable quality available in reading an earlier novel of Lish's, *Dear Mr. Capote*. In that novel, Lish placed himself in the mind and heart of a deranged killer and produced an engaging epistolary novel.

My hunch is that *Extravaganza* is pretty good but it is hard in the end to know *how* good it is.

"DIRTY" WORDS AND RESEARCH

Classic American Graffiti: Lexical Evidence from Folk Epigraphy in Western North America, a Glossarial Study of the Low Element in the English Vocabulary, by Allen Walker Read, Maledicta Press, 1977

Though in England the *1811 Dictionary of the Vulgar Tongue* had long been an underground classic, it was not until Allen Walker Read's privately printed study, this present work, was published at his own expense in Paris in 1935 that lexicographers and other researchers could examine a published document of American folk epigraphy. In 1950 Hyman E. Goldin, Frank O'Leary, and Morris Lipsius published the *Dictionary of American Underworld Lingo*. Though it is a valuable work, it is as guilty as the then current standard dictionaries of omitting the controversial folk words (such as fuck) that Read, fifteen years earlier, had carefully documented. Even then Read believed that he was making not only a valuable contribution to linguistics but was at the same time providing source material for other disciplines such as abnormal psychology. Another important work that also sidesteps most of the so-called dirty words documented by Read is *A Dictionary of the Underworld,* compiled by Eric Patridge and published in 1949.

Though Read's preface and introduction are overly defensive and somewhat apologetic he nevertheless makes solid, useful comments on the nature of obscenity and folk epigraphy. After reminding us that "The determinant of obscenity lies not in words or things, but in the attitudes that people have towards these words and things," (p. 9) he goes on to another important point: "The stigma on the obscene words was caused in the first place by unhealthy attitudes towards the bodily functions." (p. 16) After a plea for a sane sense of the body and sex, Read laments: "Being normal in the world today consists in having the neuroses that most other people have." (p. 16)

Read's innovative reflections on American folk epigraphy firmly support the seriousness of his work. He cites the rock carvings of the Conquistadors at El Moro as being perhaps the first examples of folk epigraphy in the new world. Going back to classical times he gives examples of its existence in ancient Greece, Rome, and Pompeii. "The practice was alive also in eighteenth-century England." (p. 22)

For his research Read confined his study to the United States west of the Mississippi and to the Canadian Rocky Mountain area. He discovered that the best repositories of folk epigraphy in those areas were picnic and tourist parks, toilets, and public statues. He established the fact that there was a correlation between "distinctive" inscriptions and poorly maintained repositories. He concluded that the nature of the writings and drawings examined generally reflected its character-istics in states across the nation. He also found little differences between the American "Low Element in the English Vocabulary" and examples later examined in England. Read did the research without going out of his way during the fall of 1928 and early in January of the following year. His initial effort to publish the findings in a German scholarly periodical was met with rejection.

Deciphering these messages had its problems. Farmost among them was the "illegible handwriting." Read took a few liberties in the interest of clarity but kept the original spellings and punctuation. When a word was not clear he used asterisks to indicate undecipherability.

In his "Glossary of Stigmatized Words" he explores the linguis-tic histories of forty-eight of the most taboo words in the American language. He gives brief histories of derivative terms stemming from these primary words. Among the words explored are: "bitch," "bullshit," "cock," "hole," and "jazz," of which he says: "It is unde-termined whether the original sense was music of a peculiar rhythm, or copulation. The latter is commonly believed in the Middle West." (p. 62) Read found "jazz" used both as a verb and a noun in Island Park, Cedar Falls, Iowa. The noun use of it repre-sented sperm.

Following the brave and pioneering glossary there is an "Afterword" by Reinhold Aman who praises the work as the classic that it is and says, "the graffiti collected in these pages are among the funniest of all folk speech recorded." (p. 85) Though I personally missed the humor I agree with Aman that "snide bluenoses" are everywhere. They are likely to be shocked by Dr. Read's book.

When the work first appeared in its limited edition it did surprisingly receive some serious critical consideration in several journals. Examples: *Quarterly Review of Biology:* ". . . a record, of permanent historical value, of the current American fashions in obscene inscriptions." (p. 86) *Language* said: "To the linguist the terms show interesting semantic changes, either the use of the inoffensive words to express taboo terms, or the remodeling of the offensive words so that they will somehow give the meaning without giving the offense." (p. 86) *American Speech:* ". . . all dictionaries . . . are written to satisfy the needs of certain groups in society, not to present a complete picture of language at a given time . . . they have continued to omit the vulgar words which are colloquially the most commonly used in the language. . . . The many collectors of 'slang' and students of popular English . . . will appreciate the impulse that leads Mr. Read to put down what most people do not like to see in print." (p. 89)

Allen Walker Read, born in 1906, is a distinguished scholar who has worked on many important projects, among them the *Encyclopaedia Britannica,* the *Random House Dictionary,* the Funk & Wagnalls dictionaries, and the *Dictionary of American English on Historical Principles.* This 1977 Maledicta Press edition of the original of seventy-five copies is most welcomed to our not-so-liberated times.

AMERICA PLACED ON TRIAL

The Evidence of Things Not Seen
by James Baldwin, Holt, Rinehart & Winston, 1985

Earlier in his career James Baldwin declared his right to criticize his country because of his love for it. With the essay, "The Evidence of Things Not Seen," he is exercising that right with vigor.

The book professes to be about the widely known Atlanta child murders. While in Atlanta gathering information about them, Baldwin spoke with the families of some of the victims, with a number of emergency fundraisers, with Mayor Andrew Young, and with the parents of Wayne Williams, the man accused of committing the crimes.

In the end Baldwin smelled a rat and concluded that Williams himself had to be added to "the list of Atlanta's slaughtered black children," because he was tried in a court by people ill-equipped to examine the evidence. A country that believed in the guilt of the Rosenbergs wasn't equipped to examine any evidence at all, he contends.

In other words, Baldwin puts the entire country on trial.

But the book isn't really about the murders. They serve as a vehicle on which the distinguished author rides through a much larger territory examining race relations and the human condition itself throughout the world.

Although examples of gross racial injustice in Africa and Europe are cited, it is American hypocrisy that Baldwin is primarily interested in defining and exposing. For him, the most hypocritical aspect of the American experience involves the institutionalization of whiteness as a cultural value and the oppression of black people on the basis of color.

No question about it: Racism still exists in America, despite some conservative claims to the contrary. What Baldwin's blasting essay does is to remind us that its roots are still deeply embedded here in our society, and in the concept of race itself.

Baldwin says that not only are black people still considered "niggers" by most white Americans, but that black families too often unintentionally cooperate with the system of racism by raising black boys, for example, to be docile. This state of mind in the South, Baldwin reminds us, is called "sorriness." This cooperation Baldwin sees as "the most crucial and anguished aspect of the black American reality."

In an attempt to correct some misconceptions, Baldwin states that "the black demand was not for integration" in the 1950s but for "desegregation." Baldwin suggests that, for white Americans, integration as a goal for black people meant that blacks wanted to become white. White Americans, he insists, cannot imagine anyone on earth not wanting to be white. Given this state of mind, Baldwin sees the white American as history's most "abject victim."

Baldwin's whole thesis argues that America was founded on lies, and these lies had to do with the unwillingness of the settlers to recognize the humanity of their slaves. The situation created a state of terror for black people. Baldwin says: "We all came here as candidates for the slaughter of the innocents." White people, like black people, were enslaved by the institution of slavery and the subsequent pattern of racism.

Misconceptions, Baldwin goes on to say, have shamelessly been instituted not only by America but by its entire family of Western nations—and all in the interest of maintaining the status quo where black and Third World people generally are concerned.

He compares the racial situation in South Africa to that in North America. Although managed in different ways, the racial status quo is maintained politically in both places, he suggests.

And what is so important about keeping "the existing state"? Well, it ensures profit, but Baldwin believes this kind of emphasis leads humanity in a dangerous direction: "Man cannot live by profit alone."

None of these are new arguments.

However Baldwin says, or suggests, that humanity is in a great state of social and moral and perhaps biological change, after only now beginning to recover from "the most momentous diaspora in human memory, to discover and recognize each other." This change, he says, cannot be stopped. With it, he hopes "the utterly intolerable night-mare of the American Dream" will be eroded.

"This is a global matter," he says. "This encounter will be bloody and severe: precisely because it demolishes the morality, to say noth-ing of the definitions of the Western world."

The mood of this book isn't so much that of anger as that of a broken heart. At times the reader feels that the author's despair is too heavy for him to carry alone. Yet, Baldwin's spirit is an American spirit and that, ironically, makes his arguments sound like a family fight.

And of course they do represent family fights since, as he used to say, black and white people in this country are kissing cousins, no mat-ter how sternly some may choose to deny it. But all of this may partly explain why Baldwin has for more than thirty years been such a popu-lar literary figure in his own country and, incidentally, in those coun-tries he says are helping America maintain the undesirable status quo that seems to serve only greed.

The book also serves as an occasion for Baldwin to reflect on his own childhood. He says a lot about Harlem, the early years, the mid-dle class on Sugar Hill, his teachers, his hatred for whites and his growth from that, his growing awareness of racism, leaving the church, and his personal struggle as a sensitive person attempting to come to terms with having been born into poverty and a grim situation.

Like Baldwin's earlier essays, "The Evidence of Things Not Seen" rambles the way an old mountain stream does. Stylistically Baldwin remains closer to Henry James than to, say, D.H. Lawrence, although his passion and preacherliness remind one of Lawrence at his most didactic. It is refreshing, however, to read Baldwin, especially because his terminology doesn't suffer much from the fadism influence. His vocabulary is decked with the good old-fashioned words of ritual and morality, such as sin, love, death, salvation, terror, and honor.

James Baldwin's arguments are serious ones, and this book should be read by anyone concerned with the fragile state of humanity. Although it is possible a great number of potential readers may not agree with him and may not be able to accept the bleakest aspects of his vision, no person of goodwill who has hope can afford to ignore what he has to say.

ACKNOWLEDGMENTS

END NOTES

LOOKING AT THE *DIAL:*

1. "The *Dial* (of Chicago and New York)," *A History of American Literary Magazines,* 4 vols. (Cambridge, MA: Belknap Press of Harvard University Press, 1957), 3:541.

2. Nicholas Joost, *Years of Transition: The* Dial, *1912-1920* (Barre, MA: Barre Publishers, 1967), p. 56.

3. Frederick J. Hoffman, Charles Alle, and Carolyn F. Ulrich, *The Little Magazine: A History and a Bibliography* (Princeton, NJ: Princeton University Press, 1947), p. 235.

4. S. Foster Damon, *Amy Lowell: A Chronicle* (Boston: Houghton Mifflin, 1935), p. 519.

5. Joost, p. 268.

6. Joost, pp. 96-97. See also Gerald Lacey, *D.H. Lawrence: Letters to Thomas & Adele Seltzer* (Santa Barbara, CA: Black Sparrow Press, 1976), p. 37; and Adele Seltzer's publicity pamphlet, *D.H. Lawrence: The Man and His Work* (New York: Thomas Seltzer, 1922).

CONSIDERING THE *YALE REVIEW:*

1. Frank Luther Mott, "The *Yale Review*," *A History of American Literary Magazines,* 5 vols. (Cambridge, MA: Belknap Press of Harvard University Press, 1968), 5:329.

2. Mott, 5:331.

3. Wilbur Cross, *Connecticut Yankee* (New Haven, CT: Yale University Press, 1943), pp. 187-88.

4. Ibid, p. 188.

5. Doris Ulmann, *A Portrait Gallery of American Editors* (New York: William Edwin Rudge, 1925), pp. 34-37.

6. Cross, pp. 190, 193.

7. Cross, pp. 190-191, 198.

8. According to Mott, MacAfee joined the staff as managing editor in 1925. He does not make it clear that she had been on the staff since 1912.

9. Cross, p. 199.

10. Letter received from Kai T. Erikson, February 26, 1984.

11. Erikson.

THE *LITTLE REVIEW* IN FOCUS:

1. Margaret Anderson, *My Thirty Year War; The Autobiography: Beginnings and Battles to 1930* (New York: Horizon Press, 1969), p. 65. All further references to this source will be cited in the text. Frank Luther Mott (in *A History of American Magazines,* 5 vols., Cambridge, MA: Belknap Press of Harvard University Press, 1968), 5:166, states that "Margaret Anderson escaped from her home town . . . in 1912." This does not agree with the time of her arrival in Chicago given in her autobiography.

2. Paula R. Feldman, "Margaret Anderson," *Dictionary of Literary Biography Volume 4: American Writers in Paris 1920-1939* (Detroit, MI: Gale Research Company, 1980), p. 3.

3. Nicholas Joost, *Years of Transition: The Dial, 1912-1920: An Illustrated History* (Barre, MA: Barre Publishers, 1967), p. 26.

4. Bernard Duffey, *The Chicago Renaissance in American Letters* (East Lansing: Michigan State College Press, 1954), p. 244.

5. Feldman, p. 3.

6. Mott, 5:167; Duffey, p. 246.

7. *The Little Review Anthology,* ed. Margaret Anderson (New York: Hermitage House, 1953) pp. 13, 62-63.

8. Ibid, p. 98.

9. Ezra Pound, *Selected Letters 1907–1941* (New York: New Directions, 1950), pp. 106-134.

10. Feldman, p. 5.

11. *The Little Review Anthology,* p. 329.

12. Feldman, p. 6.

13. Margaret Anderson, *The Strange Necessity; The Autobiography: Resolutions and Reminiscence to 1969* (New York: Horizon Press, 1969), p. 142.

14. Ibid, p. 149.

15. *The Little Review Anthology,* p. 353.

O   4/09